革命不是請客吃飯

A REVOLUTION IS NOT A DINNER PARTY

RICHARD H. SOLOMON

with the collaboration of
TALBOTT W. HUEY

A FEAST OF IMAGES
OF THE
MAOIST TRANSFORMATION
OF CHINA

ANCHOR PRESS • DOUBLEDAY
GARDEN CITY, NEW YORK • 1975

Library of Congress Cataloging in Publication Data

Solomon, Richard H.   1937–
A Revolution Is Not a Dinner Party

Includes bibliographical references.
1. China—Politics and government—1949–   I. Huey, Talbott W., joint author.   II. Title.
DS777.55.S617   951.05
ISBN: 0-385-09665-8
Library of Congress Catalog Card Number 74–25123

CONTENTS

Mything

the Point .1

What is the China in *your* head? If you are like most Americans, your concept of this distant but fascinating country is a jumble of fragmented and often contradictory images and themes built up by our newspapers, TV, and movies, occasional contact with someone who has traveled to China, and casual exposure to the life of Chinese living in America. Such images might well be termed myths, for at best they are simplifications of Chinese reality. More likely, they miss the point of life as a Chinese experiences it, inasmuch as they try to reduce to American terms a very different and complex society and cultural tradition.

Take, for example, a recent advertising poster: "You don't have to be Jewish to love Levy's." Most Americans experience China through their neighborhood Chinese

You don't have to be Jewish

to love Levy's
real Jewish Rye

restaurants, and know that the Chinese have developed one of the world's great cuisines. The ad thus reinforces an ethnic stereotype which identifies Chinese with fine food, conveying to at least some observers the message that, if a Chinese appreciates a European-style rye bread, the bread must be especially good. In thus mixing cultural metaphors, our mass media may communicate a clear message to an American audience, but in the process blind us to the more complex reality which lies behind the image. Is it a mere curiosity that Chinese appreciate fine food? Or does this most obvious aspect of their culture provide an interpretive key to understanding other dimensions of China's tradition, including her contemporary social and political revolution? Is Chairman Mao's observation that "a revolution is not a dinner party"[1] merely an appealing turn of phrase, or does it hold more profound meaning for those who would transform China's tradition?

This book explores such symbols or myths about and of China on the assumption that they *do* provide a basis for understanding a very different pattern of life—if interpreted from a Chinese rather than an American perspective. Thus, the following chapters combine images of China familiar to Americans into interpretive themes which seek to give them meaning in a Chinese context. Insight, however, proceeds from self-awareness. Hence, our study begins by exploring the myths which Americans hold about China. In an understanding of our own cultural biases lie points of contrast which will help us appreciate Chinese views of themselves, of their history and revolution, and of America.

CHINAS "GOOD" AND "BAD"

American images of China began to be formed when our country was little more than a cluster of British colonies, and even before. The European world had long known of an exotic land to the east. (Note that we still refer to China as "the East," although its saliency in American history has always been from the West.) Perhaps the first Western "folk memories" of China came from the voyages of Marco Polo to the court of the Mongol emperor of China in the late thirteenth century. Noodles and ravioli endure in our cuisine as fruits

of Polo's fascination with Chinese life, and as an early example of Westerners borrowing from this ancient culture. The spices and silks of Cathay were treasures which lured many of Europe's explorers in the fifteenth and sixteenth centuries—including Columbus, whose voyage led to the discovery of America. In the European "Enlightenment" of the eighteenth century, things Chinese were a passion with the educated classes. Tea and silks became indispensable amenities in the life of the rich. Furniture designed in pseudo-Chinese style (like Chippendale) brought cabinet craft to new heights of artistry.

Intellectually, there was a corresponding tendency to idealize those fragments of Chinese life brought back by traders and missionaries. In social and political terms, the stereotype of Cathay took the form of grave, wise, cultivated Confucian gentlemen called "mandarins" who presided grandly over a realm that seemed to have achieved what the feuding states of Europe in the 1700s could not: political unity and moral harmony. China's political tradition was to influence the development of our own governmental institutions as first the British, and then the Americans, established civil service systems patterned on the centuries-old Chinese imperial examinations. Such early American leaders as Franklin and Jefferson saw in China a populous and prosperous society graced with a thriving economy and governed by an educated elite, a model for their own newly founded nation.

Inevitably, however, the pendulum had to swing in the other direction. As the West learned more of actual conditions in China, and as the Ch'ing empire succumbed to the peasant rebellions, leadership feuds and foreign interventions of the 1800s, the exotic and cultured "Middle Kingdom" was transformed into the "sick man of Asia."

"Could we be so fortunate as to introduce the industry of the Chinese, their arts of living and improvements in husbandry . . . America might become in time as populous as China."
—American Philosophical Society, 1768.[2]

After China's defeat by the British in the Opium War of 1839–42 —so called because what was at stake was the ability of the Chinese government to resist the British introduction of opium into the country as a medium of trade—the earlier admiration with which the West viewed China turned to disdain for her inept weakness and the venal conservatism of her officials. "A sudden revulsion of feeling took place, and from being respected and admired, China's utter collapse before British arms and her unwillingness to receive Western intercourse and ideals led to a feeling of contempt. . . . The impression spread through America and Europe that China was decadent, dying, falling greatly from her glorious past."[3] In contrast to the enthusiasm for China of the Jesuits, who had been received with respect during the seventeenth century at the courts of late Ming and early Ch'ing dynasty emperors, Protestant evangelists of the 1800s were appalled by the poverty of the common people and the violence (at times officially inspired) with which their missionary efforts were received, and dismayed by the manner in which Christian doctrine was distorted by its Chinese adherents.

Illustrative of the disillusionment which had come over American contacts with China was the book *Chinese Characteristics,* published in 1894 by the missionary Arthur Smith. While Smith found admirable qualities of politeness, patience, and good humor in the people he sought to convert, his writings reveal deep frustration with other characteristics of suspiciousness, insincerity, intellectual turbidity, and contempt for foreigners. Smith's difficulty in comprehending the ways of the Chinese he lived among was perhaps best revealed in his attribution of their ability to bear life's hardships and suffering to "an absence of nerves."[4]

Thus, as the 1800s drew to a close, American attitudes toward China had gone through a cycle from ill-informed enthusiasm to disappointment—a pattern that was to be repeated more than once in the twentieth century.

The nineteenth century also saw the creation of particular American stereotypes of China derived from the arrival within the United States of a growing population of Chinese immigrants. Coming from impoverished coastal areas of South China in the 1850s and '60s as contract laborers to help build America's railroads and dig for California gold, the Chinese were the most alien of the ethnic newcomers

by solid Anglo-Saxon standards. Their curious dress and hair style, strange cuisine, and opaque language compounded the inability (or noninclination) of white Americans to understand why the Chinese behaved as they did. Moreover, the ease in "cowboy America" with which powerless immigrants could be persecuted drove the instinctively clannish Chinese into isolated and defensive urban ghettoes.

What may have been most exasperating to other Americans was the natural instinct the Chinese seemed to have for the middle-class entrepreneurial game: they were desperately hard workers in their hand laundries and restaurants, as frugal as any Scotsman could wish, shrewd in their business dealings, and would have made sober and law-abiding citizens had they not been denied citizenship on racial grounds. Perhaps as a result of this disturbing combination of the foreign and the threateningly adaptive, the Chinese immigrant became "a familiar curiosity, in turn welcomed, patronized, mocked, feared, hated, lynched, excluded, ignored, tolerated, liked—oddly feared or oddly admired, but scarcely ever known, understood, or simply accepted."[5]

In their relations with the real China across the sea, Americans of the generations following the pioneers of the China trade tended to fall into a few standard roles: soldier, missionary, merchant, and educator. European powers and the United States quickly obtained special privileges and concessions from the powerless Manchu court in Peking, which enabled them to carry on commercializing, Christianizing, and at times brutalizing the Chinese with impunity. At the same

time, in the United States the federal and state governments moved to discriminate legally against Chinese immigrants, giving implicit sanction to rampant racism. The Chinese Exclusion Act, passed by Congress in 1882, formally expressed American fears of the hard-working but incomprehensible Chinese immigrant in a period of economic recession, and legitimated sporadic acts of violence per-

THEY ARE PRETTY SAFE THERE.

When Politicians do Agree, their Unanimity is Wonderful.

"GIVE IT TO HIM, HE'S GOT NO VOTE NOR NO FRIENDS!"

petrated on hapless Chinese, as has been recorded in the writings of such major literary figures as Bret Harte and Mark Twain.

The images of Chinese in America and in distant China have tended to blend phantasmagorically over the years. The "Chinatown" ghettoes of America came to be associated by the popular maga-zines with images of mystery and cruelty consonant with what Ameri-cans felt and feared about "inscrutable" Chinese in China:

> The mystery of Chinatown was suggested by a whole series of visual cliches—the ominous shadow of an Oriental figure thrown against a wall, secret panels which slide back to reveal an inscrutable Oriental face, the huge shadow of a hand with tapering fingers and long pointed fingernails poised menacingly, the raised dagger appearing suddenly and unexpectedly from between closed curtains.[6]

Out of such pop-culture nightmares grew that sinister figure Dr. Fu Manchu, first a novelistic character, then the villain-hero of a series of films. "He was revengeful, merciless, adept at obscure forms of slow torture, a master of unknown drugs, and the lord of a vast army of thugs and slaves ready to do his worst bidding. He was so evil that he periodically had to be killed off, and was so mysteriously superpowerful that he always miraculously reappeared in time for the next episode."[7]

In the period of the 1920s and 1930s the image of the "bad" Chinese symbolized by Fu Manchu reached a crest and then began to recede. In symbolic terms, the "wily evil" of Dr. Fu came to be

countered by the "wily virtue" of another fictional Chinese-American
—the Honolulu detective Charlie Chan. "Charlie," as he was referred
to despite his years and quiet dignity, was "blandly humble in the
face of Occidental contempt and invariably confounded all concerned
by his shrewd solution of the crime. His aphorisms, always preceded
by 'Confucius say—,' passed into the national vernacular, along with
pseudo-Chinese terms like 'Number One Son.'"[8] Charlie Chan's dig-
nified reserve and esoteric talents for coping with adversity endure
in America's contemporary media in the TV series "Kung Fu," even
while images of the violent and evil Chinese persist in newspaper and
school-text characterizations of Chinese Communism.[9]

THE OPEN DOOR
TO COMMERCE, CHRISTIANITY, AND CHAOS

On the international scene, Sino-American relations in the twentieth century began with the creation of some of the more powerful and enduring myths affecting our perceptions of China. The turn of the century was a period of growing rivalry between the industrializing states of Europe, Japan, and the United States. A worldwide scramble for colonial possessions led even independence-minded Americans to acquire the Philippines as a dependent territory in 1898; and both government officials and businessmen feared American exclusion from China by the British, French, and other foreign powers whose gunboats had established spheres of influence in the moribund Middle Kingdom.

In these circumstances, Secretary of State John Hay initiated a series of diplomatic exchanges in 1899 and 1900 addressed to the world powers seeking their commitment to the principle of the "territorial and administrative integrity" of China, as well as to the right of all countries to trade in the foreign enclaves that had been established at Shanghai and other "treaty ports." Hay's efforts to maintain for the U.S. an "open door" to China drew only vague expressions of support from the Japanese, British, Russians, and other contending powers; yet it established in American minds a sense that we had a special responsibility to protect China's interests in a predatory world —even as our own businessmen pursued an elusive search for 400 million customers, and while our missionaries dedicated themselves to the salvation of Chinese souls.

Within China, reaction to the unwanted alien presence which came through the open door took the form of a xenophobic popular uprising against the foreign diplomatic community and Chinese converts to Christianity. Originating in the last years of the nineteenth century as a rebellious secret society, the "Righteous Harmonious Fists"—or "Boxers," as foreigners called them—were encouraged by the tottering Ch'ing court to attack the Westerners and Chinese attracted to their ways. The Boxer rioting of 1900, which took the lives of the German Minister to Peking, several hundred foreign missionaries, and thousands of their Chinese converts, culminated in a two-month-long siege of the Diplomatic Quarter in Peking. An eight-nation expeditionary force, including several hundred American marines, was dispatched to the Chinese capital to put down the

Body of American artillery captain, killed during Boxer Rebellion,
surrounded by his men

uprising. The recalcitrant Ch'ing court was duly punished by the foreign troops, who burned and looted the imperial palaces.

Insult was then added to injury when the intervening powers demanded compensation from the Chinese government for the expense and loss of life incurred in restoring order. The Manchus, having neither the troops to defend China's interests nor the experience at the Westerners' diplomatic game to prevent the imposition of an indem-

"PING PONG";
OR, "A GAME THAT HE *DOES* UNDERSTAND."

nity, reluctantly agreed to pay the foreign powers $300 million for their intervention, thus mortgaging the country's customs revenues from international commerce for years to come.

Uneasy with the manner in which the Boxer indemnity had been acquired, the American government converted its share of the funds into a scholarship program for the education of Chinese students in the United States. Thus official policy helped to develop a sense of patronizing righteousness about American intentions toward China which was basic to what one author has termed the "Age of Benevolence" in Sino-American relations in the first decades of this century.[10]

Embodied in the Open Door policy and the Boxer Rebellion, however, were contradictions which have complicated our view of China and the reality of her revolution. Americans developed a special sense of friendship and responsibility for the Chinese people; yet when such sentiments were not reciprocated with Yankee enthusiasm on the part of the Chinese, our good will has turned to disappointment and at times to a bitter sense of rejection. This was to be most notably the case after the American "loss of China" to Communism in 1949.

We enthusiastically exported our culture to China—our commerce and technology, educational system, and religion—without appreciating how in doing so we were undermining for Chinese their sense of tradition and their self-respect. It is only belatedly that we have come to see the irony in the way our educators, evangelists, businessmen, and soldiers helped to stimulate China's twentieth-century revolution —most notably the Chinese Communist movement. The Party was founded in 1921 by students who had been exposed to "agitators" of the YMCA movement and the educational innovations of John Dewey and Bertrand Russell, as well as to Lenin's theory of imperialism. These hopeful young revolutionaries met in the safety of the foreign quarter of commercial Shanghai, living in the dormitory of a French girls' school as they plotted ways to drive the foreigners from their country and overturn the rule of China's bourgeoisie.

PEARL BUCK'S PEASANTS
AND EDGAR SNOW'S REBEL HEROES

Among the phenomena of the "Age of Benevolence" which exerted a major influence on American perceptions of China were two books written in the 1930s, one by the daughter of a missionary and the other by an aspiring young journalist passing through Shanghai on a world tour. *The Good Earth,* Pearl Buck's novel published in 1931, gave readers of the English language more information about the daily life of China's peasants—to this day more than 80 per cent of the population—than any other written work up to that time. The novel was a runaway best-seller of more than two million copies and won for its author the Nobel Prize in literature. Subsequently the book was turned into a motion picture that reached a worldwide audience of tens of millions more. (The film, it might be noted, featured heavily made-up Occidentals in the leading roles—not Chinese.) Pearl Buck's sympathetic, down-to-earth characterizations of the peasant Wang Lung and his wife O-lan, her description of the terrible pressures under which they lived, gave Americans an entirely new way to visualize the Chinese: simple, appealing, understandable folk who were admirable underdogs in a lifelong struggle against mandarin and merchant, the vagaries of nature, even fate itself.

Pearl Buck had been brought up with a curiously significant attitude toward the Chinese. Of her childhood as a missionary daughter she wrote, "I had a few dolls, but my 'children' were the small folk of the servants' quarters and the neighbors and we had wonderful hours of play."[11] This maternal if implicitly condescending attitude found wide expression in America in the 1930s, in Sunday church collections for the "starving Chinese," and in a renewed concern—heightened by Japan's forcible establishment of a puppet state in Manchuria in 1932—for the security of China and her people.

A counterpoint to *The Good Earth* was Edgar Snow's journalistic coup *Red Star Over China,* published in 1938. In an era when fear of the "Red menace" of Communism heavily influenced American responses to world events, Snow's humanizing description of the leaders of the Chinese Communist movement, just struggling to overcome the rigors of the Long March and preparing for war against Japan, gave Americans their first sympathetic picture of the revolutionary movement which was to come to power in China a decade later. Snow had come to China in 1928 for a brief visit, but remained as a reporter for such magazines as *Life* and the *Saturday Evening Post*. In Peking he befriended Chinese students associated with the Communist underground who eventually helped him make his way through Japanese and Nationalist Chinese blockades to the Communist base area at Yenan, in the desolate northwest province of Shensi. His interviews with Mao Tse-tung, Chou En-lai, and other

Edgar Snow with Mao Tse-tung
in northern Shensi Province, 1936

Communist leaders, and his favorable description of their "rural equalitarianism," were well received in Europe and the U.S. by a public hopeful that China would resist Japanese expansionism.

As America herself became enmeshed in the war against Japan, official policy placed full support behind the Nationalist government of Chiang Kai-shek; yet Edgar Snow's favorable impression of the Chinese Communist movement was sustained by State Department and U. S. Army observers such as John Service, David Barrett, and Evans Carlson, who found the discipline and morale of Yenan an appealing contrast to the corruption and demoralization in the Nationalist's wartime capital of Chungking.

Chu Teh, John S. Service, Mao Tse-tung, and Colonel David Barrett in Yenan, 1944

When China's red star rose in 1949 with the defeat of the Nationalists in the civil war, Service and other observers sympathetic to the Communists were hounded from government service by Senator McCarthy's Cold War anti-Communist crusade. Edgar Snow and his wife, blacklisted for their left-wing sympathies, took up residence in Switzerland. With the passage of time, however, Snow's personal association with Mao Tse-tung and Chou En-lai was to provide Americans with one of their few windows on "Communist China" during two decades of Cold War confrontation, in books and journal articles published after his 1960 and 1964 trips to China through the official U.S. government travel blockade. Indeed, Snow was to be the harbinger of a new era in Sino-American relations when, in the fall of 1970, Chairman Mao brought him atop the Gate of Heavenly Peace in Peking for a National Day demonstration of renewed Sino-American friendship.

The China portrayed to the world by Edgar Snow was not, however, the China perceived by most Americans, or the strong and united ally which leaders in Washington wanted it to be. Consistently since the nineteenth century, foreign governments had placed great emphasis on the desirability of a China united under a single government strong enough to keep internal order and resist domination by any one outside power—yet not so strong or nationalistic as to exclude all foreign commercial activity or social and political involvement with the outside world. When in 1928 the Kuomintang (or Nationalist Party) leader General Chiang Kai-shek established a "Central Government" at Nanking—having either conquered or formed coalitions with the local warlord regimes that had fragmented China since the fall of the Ch'ing dynasty—many foreigners saw in him the hope of a leader who would unify the country while remaining receptive to outside influence.

Chiang had many qualities that appealed to Americans. Despite his early flirtation with the Soviet Union (he was dubbed the "Red General" after six months of military training in Russia in 1923) and attacks on foreigners associated with his rise to power, Chiang's annihilation of Chinese Communist labor unions in Shanghai in 1927

and his resistance to Soviet encroachment in Manchuria the following year established his authenticity as a nationalist and an anti-Communist. At the same time, his espousal of Sun Yat-sen's "three people's principles"—translated in the West as "nationalism" (*min-tzu*), "democracy" (*min-ch'uan*), and "popular welfare" (*min-sheng*)— seemed to hold the prospect of a China rejuvenated in terms Americans could identify with. He not only turned to the Western banking community in Shanghai for support for his new government, but in 1928 crowned his commitment to values familiar to Americans by marrying the charming Wellesley graduate Soong Mei-ling and converting to Methodism.

By the early 1930s American missionary circles and the business community were convinced that China's hope, and their own interests, lay with the Chiangs—a view that gained wide acceptance in the U.S. through the publication efforts of Henry Luce, son of an American China missionary and founder of the *Time-Life* media empire. The same year that Edgar Snow's *Red Star Over China*

TIME

The Weekly Newsmagazine

Painted for TIME *by S. J. Woolf*

MAN & WIFE OF THE YEAR
"*Any sacrifice should not be regarded as too costly.*"
(See FOREIGN NEWS)

Volume XXXI   Number 1

presented China's Communist future to the world, *Time* magazine selected Madame and Generalissimo Chiang as 1938's "Man and Wife of the Year."

American concerns about China were heightened as Japan moved beyond her 1932 conquest of Manchuria to an all-out invasion of China proper. Although Chiang Kai-shek had promoted only token resistance to Japanese actions against China's peripheral regions—preferring to concentrate his efforts against the internal Communist insurgency—by 1937 popular sentiment and the kidnapping of the Generalissimo at Sian by Manchurian troops resentful of his passive resistance to the foreign invader forced the establishment of a Nationalist-Communist "united front" against the Japanese.

As the nominal leader of China, Chiang became for Americans, and particularly for President Franklin Roosevelt, the focal point of sympathy and support for the beleaguered country. After Pearl Harbor, the United States and Nationalist China became allies in a crusade to drive Japanese imperial power from the Pacific, as was

most colorfully portrayed to Americans in the swashbuckling exploits of Claire Chennaults's Fourteenth Air Force "Flying Tigers" and efforts to supply Chiang's forces by airlift from Burma over the "hump" of the Himalayas. Already burdened by its war with Hitler's Germany on the European front, the Roosevelt Administration committed scarce material resources and its diplomatic influence to transforming Chiang's China into a modernized world power which would relieve American burdens in a two-front war and then become a bulwark of a new international order after the defeat of Germany and Japan.

Unfortunately the expectations which Americans held for the Generalissimo and his "Central Government" far surpassed the fragile unity and limited military effectiveness of his coalition of warlord and Communist forces. While Washington committed itself to Chiang in the hope that he would build an effective resistance against the Japanese invaders—and in the process establish a position for a strong China in the postwar world—the "Gimo," as the press dubbed him, saw his first priority as maintaining the strength of his own

General Joseph W. Stilwell, Madame Chiang Kai-shek, and the Generalissimo in Chungking, 1943

military units against domestic rivals for power—primarily the Communists. The colorful and caustic diaries of General Joseph Stilwell, who had been sent to China by President Roosevelt as a military adviser to Chiang and later served as Chief of Staff of the Nationalist armies, record the failure of American efforts to train China's armies into an effective fighting force. Insensitive to the manner in which military forces influenced the political balance within China, "Vinegar Joe" Stilwell railed at the repeated obstruction of his plans to build a thirty-division ground army (which would have strengthened the position of some of Chiang's rivals for power) by what he termed the "Peanut Dictator" (i.e., Chiang).[12] The bad feelings which grew between the Generalissimo and Stilwell ultimately led President Roosevelt to relieve "Vinegar Joe" of his responsibilities in China in the fall of 1944.

While Stilwell's recall deferred to Chiang Kai-shek's wishes, it did not represent a lessening of the conflicting perspectives on politics

Mao Tse-tung, Chou En-lai, General George C. Marshall, Nationalist General Chang Chih-chung, and Chu Teh in Yenan, March 1946

and military affairs which made it so difficult for Americans to deal with the realities of wartime China. This was to be brought home in even more profound ways after the defeat of Japan, first by the failure of General George Marshall's attempt to negotiate a coalition government, and thus avoid a civil war between the Nationalists and their Communist rivals in 1946, and then by the rapid defeat of Chiang's armies by the Communists between 1947 and 1949. American conceptions of compromise politics and the primacy of national goals over parochial commitments to family and faction were unable to cope with the harsh realities of Nationalist China at war.

The collapse of the Chiang government and rise to power of the Communists generated one of those great swings of public mood that have periodically characterized America's orientation to China. The sympathy and inflated admiration which had existed for the wartime ally turned to contempt and bitterness after 1949. These

sentiments were further compounded by the tales of wartime China brought back home by American soldiers and journalists who, in experiencing the tragedy of a demoralized and fragmented society, had come to believe "that all Chinese were corrupt, inefficient, unreliable," and who responded to "the squalor, filth, and ignorance . . . with loathing and revulsion."[13]

This disillusionment was further transformed into fear, when in February 1950 the new Communist government in Peking formally allied itself with the Soviet Union. America's anxieties about postwar Russian duplicity and expansionism in Europe were transferred to

John S. Service and Senator Joseph R. McCarthy departing Senate
Foreign Relations Committee hearings, June 1950

"Red China" in Asia. Senator Joseph McCarthy pressed his search for
"traitors" in the U.S. government who had duped the public into
believing that the Chinese Communists were nothing more than "agrar-
ian reformers."

Had international developments not turned so quickly to open
violence, Americans might have adjusted, with the passage of time,
to the "loss" of their largely self-created special friendship for Nationalist China. As events were to transpire, however, the onset of
the Korean War in the summer of 1950 further fueled American fears

of a global Communist conspiracy. Our perceptions of China went through a series of chromatic transformations. The "Red menace" image became the "yellow peril," as Chinese Communist soldiers entered the Korean conflict and overran ill-prepared and under-manned American defenders in "human wave" assaults. It seemed to be Genghis Khan and the "Golden Horde" reincarnated in the twentieth century. As American prisoners of war co-operated with the Communists in publicly denouncing U.S. involvement in the Korean conflict, and then returned with tales of being "brainwashed" by their Chinese captors, reality seemed to be given to the images of Oriental cruelty developed in earlier decades by the screen fantasies of Dr. Fu Manchu.

For their part, the Chinese Communists saw American intervention in Korea, and the concurrent "neutralization" of Taiwan by the U. S. Seventh Fleet, as renewed involvement in the unresolved civil war against the Nationalists and a threat to their security along the same path taken by Japan in its march from Korea to Manchuria in the 1930s. Amid conflicting charges of American "germ warfare" and Communist aggression, China and the U.S. became locked into a hostile confrontation that was to be a major feature of the Cold War political landscape.

The specter of Communist expansionism became the central theme in American foreign policy during the remainder of the 1950s and '60s. Containment and isolation of Communist China were key elements of global efforts to defend the Free World. Secretary of State John Foster Dulles was the architect of a structure of bilateral treaties and regional alliances with Korea, Japan, Taiwan, and other states with interests in the Pacific and Indochina, designed to isolate Communism in Asia. The story is still told of Dulles' encounter with China's then-Foreign Minister, Chou En-lai, at the Geneva Conference on Indochina in 1954. Confronted with the awkward presence of the representative of an unrecognized state, Dulles refused to proffer his hand to the Chinese leader—symbolically emphasizing the gulf of hostility and distrust which now separated the two countries.

Within China, the force of a profound social revolution sustained itself through the 1950s and '60s in a series of upheavals involving destruction of the landlord class, collectivization of the economy, and attacks on intellectuals. These events, seen only in vague outline by Americans from behind the "Bamboo Curtain" of confrontation and isolation, further compounded the sense of alienation between two profoundly different social and political traditions.

As the Communist Party mobilized China's "masses" in an effort to transform the life style and labor pattern of a tradition-bound peasant society, Americans could not see a people's desperate struggle for economic security, political unity, and national defense; we saw only a terrible burden of labor and mental conformity imposed on faceless "blue ants"—a journalist's phrase, derived from the look-alike work outfits worn by Chinese peasants and factory laborers,

which was well calculated to offend Americans' highly developed sense of individuality. And then during the "Cultural Revolution" of the mid-1960s—to complete the series of chromatic images—the faceless phalanxes of "blue ants" disintegrated into a bedlam of rioting Red Guards, as China's students embarked on what seemed to the outside world to be an ultimate act of madness—destruction of the very organizational core of the revolution, the Communist Party. So fixated were Americans with the image of violence-prone Chinese that even the sober New York *Times* could caption a picture of students marching with wooden guns as "Chinese Young Pioneers drilling with modern rifles."

The New York Times Book Review
JANUARY 14, 1968

Chinese Young Pioneers drilling with modern rifles.

Photograph by Marc Riboud.

MYTHS AND MISINTERPRETATIONS

These varied images of China are the myths with which Americans have interpreted the lives and history of one quarter of mankind for more than a century. While such perceptions grasp at fragments of Chinese reality, in mything the point we have often missed the point, for our views have been shaped more by American experience and values than by a distant Chinese reality. For their part, the Chinese interpret life through their own set of historical and cultural biases, which in similar fashion distort their perceptions of us. Such differences of view have given rise to international misunderstanding and the swings of mood which have been so characteristic of the history of Sino-American relations.

The following chapters of this book attempt to break down American stereotypes of China and contrast them with Chinese myths and images of China—of its changing society and political revolution. We explore cultural themes of an ancient pattern of life that is being broken by one of the great social transformations of our time. Hopefully the contrast between American and Chinese perceptions will lead to an honest appreciation of our differences, if not a clearer grasp of Chinese realities.

Eating .2

Traditional Chinese culture was shaped by a concern basic to other peasant societies where survival and subsistence were directly dependent upon yearly agricultural production: having enough food to eat. The flood plains of China's great river valleys—the Yellow and the Yangtze—were centers of a vigorous agricultural economy which over thousands of years facilitated the growth of population and a great civilization. But attendant problems of overpopulation, flood, and drought endured as basic issues shaping China's governmental institutions, the life style of peasant, merchant, and landlord, and the manner in which children were reared to deal with life's hardships. One peasant from North China, in recalling the personal suffering of a period of famine endured in

his youth, seemed to be speaking for countless generations of rural Chinese when he described his own basic preoccupation with having enough to eat, a concern born of family tragedy:

We came to Yenan from Hengshan when I was five. That was during the great famine of 1928. . . . We went about begging. . . . We had nothing to eat. Father went to Chao-chuan to gather firewood and beg food, but he didn't get any. He was carrying elmleaves and firewood when he fell by the roadside. . . . That is my earliest memory: of always being hungry, and of father there dead in the road.[1]

In a society where eating had the elemental meaning of survival, it is not surprising that the bearing of hardships came to be characterized by Chinese as "eating bitterness" (*ch'ih-k'u*), and that children were educated to cope with the frustrations and anxieties of life by "swallowing anger" and "putting it in the stomach." These are the ways Chinese describe the personal emotional discipline seen as essential for maintaining group harmony in a society where survival depended upon collective family labor.

The preoccupation with eating also shaped the life style of China's landlords and mandarins. The source of wealth and security of the society's traditional elite was based upon ownership of land. And the mandarins' concern with the preparation and eating of fine food produced in China one of the world's great culinary traditions—

known only indirectly to Americans through the neighborhood Chinese restaurant, perhaps China's most ubiquitous export to the Western world.

Explicitly emphasizing the manner in which mutual feeding was the basis of group and individual security, the ancient Confucian educational text, the *Classic of Filial Piety*, stressed the obligation of

children to feed aged parents, just as they had been fed by father and mother or grandparents in childhood. Chinese society was thus organized around the oral interdependence of the generations.

Many of the concepts of society and interpersonal relations basic to the Chinese view of the world are derived from this concern with food, eating, and survival. The Chinese vision of utopia, termed *ta-t'ung,* or "the great harmony," is basically the notion of a prosperous and unified family able to share a common meal together. The

Chinese concept of hospitality stresses inviting visitors to share a meal, and efforts to resolve interpersonal disputes in this society traditionally take place at a banquet table. The Chinese ideal of friendship is above all a group of companions united around a table over common bowls of food.

While Chinese ideas about caring and companionship stress eating, conversely their image of social conflict and aggression has been one of "consuming enemies" or "being eaten" by them. For peasants

Continued on page 40

All things in the world are divisible. Even this colossus of U.S. imperialism can be split up, it can be split up and defeated. The peoples of Asia, Africa, and Latin America, and other regions, with some hitting at its head, and some striking at its feet, can mouthful by mouthful eat it up; piece by piece destroy it.

—Lin Piao, *Long Live the*
Victory of People's War (1965)

China is an attractive piece of meat coveted by all. But this piece of meat is very tough, and for years no one has been able to bite into it. It is even more difficult now that Lin Piao the "superspy" has fallen. . . . The ambitions of the two hegemonic powers—the U.S. and the USSR—are one thing, but whether they achieve them is quite another. They want to devour China, but find it too tough even to bite. Europe and Japan are also hard to bite, not to mention the vast Third World.

—Chou En-lai, "Report to the
Tenth National Congress of the
Communist Party of China" (1973)

Continued from page 37

in a time of famine, the landlord who demanded his rental payment of grain, or the rice merchant who inflated prices or hoarded his stocks, committed an aggressive act that could result in death by starvation. Those with political power could "eat people" by commandeering through taxation life's basic sustenance: food. This "man-eating" quality of the powerful in Chinese society was perhaps most evident to peasants in the ravagings of imperial or warlord armies who lived off the land they were supposed to protect. This was described by a peasant who recalled the behavior of troops of the northern warlord Hu Tsung-nan, who came to his village in the 1920s:

When Hu Tsung-nan came, almost everyone left Liu Ling. We
went up into the hills. I was in the people's militia then. We had
buried all our possessions and all our corn. Hu Tsung-nan destroyed everything, and his troops ate and ate. They discovered
our grain stores, and they stole our cattle.[2]

Such experiences lead Chinese to characterize an unjust government as more fearsome than a man-eating tiger. This was expressed
for generations in the Confucian parable of the old woman who
chose to live in the mountain wilds of her native Shantung Province
despite the fact that her son, husband, and father-in-law had been
eaten by tigers, for there was no oppressive government in her desolate
home region.

In passing by the side of Mount Thai, Confucius came on a woman who was wailing bitterly by a grave. The Master . . . sent Tze-lu to question her. "Your wailing," said he, "is altogether like that of one who has suffered sorrow upon sorrow." She replied, "It is so. Formerly, my husband's father was killed here by a tiger. My husband was also killed [by another], and now my son has died in the same way." The Master said, "Why do you not leave the place?" The answer was, "There is no oppressive government here."

—The Book of Rites

A basic aspect of revolutionary change in twentieth-century China has been the effort of young intellectuals to break away from the oral and dependent traditions of the old society. The radical author Lu Hsun, writing in 1918, attacked the demanding and submissive doctrine of filial piety which he saw as the ideological cornerstone of China's ancient "man-eating" society. Lu Hsun described how the obligations of service to parents "ate up" the lives of filial children:

I remember when I was four or five years old, sitting in the cool of the hall, my brother told me that if a man's parents were ill, he should cut off a piece of his flesh and boil it for them if he wanted to be considered a good son. . . . I have only just realized that I have been living all these years in a place where for four thousand years they have been eating human flesh.[3]

Dissatisfaction with the restrictions of traditional family life led many educated young Chinese at the turn of the century to seek ways of modernizing their society. Mao Tse-tung was one of numerous students alienated from the old way of life; but unlike many of his contemporaries Mao was sensitive to the social roots of China's political order. While still a high-school student he saw the potential for revolution in popular discontent with an imperial government that would not feed its people in a time of starvation:

There had been a severe famine . . . and in Changsha thousands were without food. The starving sent a delegation to the civil governor to beg for relief, but he replied to them haughtily, "Why haven't you food? There is plenty in the city. I always have

enough." When the people were told the governor's reply, they became very angry. They held mass meetings and organized a demonstration. They attacked the Manchu yamen, cut down the flagpole, the symbol of office, and drove out the governor. . . . A new governor arrived, and at once ordered the arrest of the leaders of the uprising. Many of them were beheaded and their heads displayed on poles as a warning to future "rebels."

This incident was discussed in my school for many days. It made a deep impression on me. Most of the other students sympathized with the "insurrectionists," but only from an observer's point of view. They did not understand that it had any relation to their own lives. They were merely interested in it as an exciting incident. I never forgot it. I felt that there with the rebels were ordinary people like my own family and I deeply resented the injustice of the treatment given to them.[4]

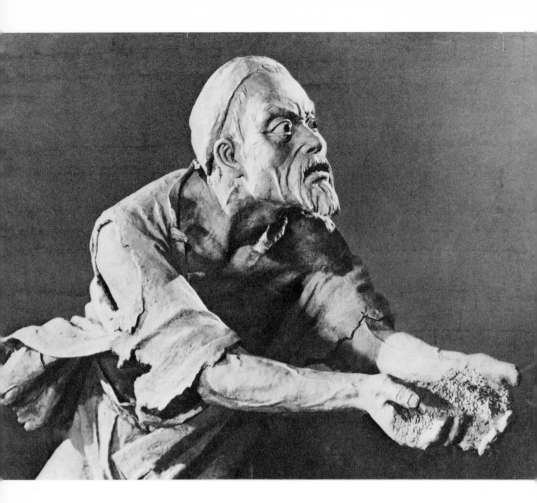

From this experience Mao gained a sense of popular discontent with the existing order of things. The problem was how to sustain and direct such mass anger in support of a social revolution. Mao's rural upbringing made him aware of the tendency of the peasants to avoid political involvement, and their inclination to "eat the bitterness" of life's hardships and injustice. But he also knew of China's long tradition of peasant rebellions. His solution to this problem of how to involve a basically conservative and apolitical rural population in a revolution which would completely reshape peasant life developed only after years of effort to organize support for the Communist movement in the Chinese countryside.

In the 1930s Mao came to see a way of encouraging the peasants to liberate their resentments against social and political injustice and to struggle against the old way of life. Whereas the Confucian manda-

rins for centuries had taught China's people to "swallow their bitterness," Mao conceived of "speak bitterness" rallies in which the peasants were urged by Party cadres to express their resentments against "class enemies," to "vomit the bitter water" of hardship, and to work up a rage against exploitation and injustice by landlord, magistrate, and foreign invader. With feelings of hatred roused, the confining routine of rural life was broken, and peasants became willing fighters for Mao's proletarian revolution. By absorbing into the ranks of the Party and the Red Army a rural population disaffected with the rival Nationalist government and fearful of the brutality of Japanese invaders, Mao built an army which—as he later described it to Party leaders—had the power to "eat up" Chiang Kai-shek's Nationalists, the Kuomintang, which he ridiculed as being a mere "paper tiger,"[5] incapable of eating anyone:

[Political] synthesis is a matter of eating one's enemy. How did we synthesize the Kuomintang? Didn't we take in things captured from the enemy and transform them! We didn't just kill captured enemy soldiers. Some of them we let go, but the large part we absorbed into our ranks. Weapons, provisions, and all kinds of things were taken in. What was of no use we eliminated, to use a philosophical term. . . . Eating is both analysis and synthesis. Take eating crabs for example. You eat the meat and not the shell. One's stomach absorbs the nourishment and expels the waste. . . . Synthesizing the Kuomintang was a matter of eating it up, absorbing most of it and expelling a smaller part.[6]

After the establishment of the People's Republic in 1949, Mao Tse-tung's efforts to transform the customs and habits of Chinese society were often expressed in the images of its enduring oral traditions. On the eve of victory in the civil war Mao warned Party leaders of the dangers of the revolutionary will of Party members being corrupted by eating "sugar-coated bullets":

> With victory, the people will be grateful to us and the bourgeoisie will come forward to flatter us. It has been proved that the enemy cannot conquer us by force of arms. However, the flattery of the bourgeoisie may conquer the weak-willed in our ranks. There may be some Communists, who were not conquered by enemies with guns and were worthy of the name of heroes for standing up to these enemies, but who cannot withstand sugar-coated bullets; they will be defeated by sugar-coated bullets. We must guard against such a situation.[7]

Mao Tse-tung and P'eng Chen, Mayor of Peking, 1958

Mao's warning reflected his perception that the elitism of the old mandarin scholar-officials was derived from their eating in affluent leisure the fruits of peasant labor. To prevent such corruption of the Party's proletarian cadres, Mao instituted on several occasions after 1949 *hsia-fang,* or "transfer downward," campaigns, in which Party and government officials would leave their offices to participate in productive labor in factories or on farms in order to sustain working-class discipline and thwart tendencies toward bureaucracy and elitism.

Efforts to transform the life style of China's peasants also focused on the production and consumption of food. In order to overcome the fragmented, family-centered quality of rural society, Mao urged the Party to organize the peasantry into large collective units of production

which would help realize the goal of a socialized economy. During the early 1950s, the traditional Chinese family farming unit was gradually replaced by neighborhood Mutual Aid Teams, then by basic-level Agricultural Producers' Cooperatives, which united the labor power of small villages, and in 1955 with advanced Cooperatives, which brought together as many as three hundred peasant households for collective labor. This process of socializing the rural economy culminated in 1958 with the formation of People's Communes, which amalgamated whole townships with tens of thousands of inhabitants into collective agricultural units. An important element of the Communes, which were promoted as a way of breaking down remaining "feudal" attitudes of the peasantry and sustaining their mobilization for collective labor, was the formation of public mess halls. If people ate together as "production teams," went the theory, then the emotional focus of their lives would be more likely to shift from the traditional parochial commitments of family and clan to those of local community and nation.

The Great Leap Forward of 1958–60, with the People's Commune as its central institution, was a heroic effort to break China out of the bonds of traditional rural social organization and ancient patterns of agricultural production, and to place the country firmly on the road to national development and social progress. Through this mass campaign Mao Tse-tung sought to convince the Chinese people that, as had been the case with the Party's rapid defeat of the Nationalists in the civil war, mobilized popular effort could now overcome all domestic and foreign impediments to the country's modernization. Explicitly symbolizing this conviction was the Great Leap propaganda campaign ridiculing China's then major international opponent, the United States—personified in the figure of Secretary of State John Foster Dulles—as nothing more than a paper tiger which, like the Nationalists and China's economic problems, could be exposed and vanquished through collective struggle. The Great Leap was Mao

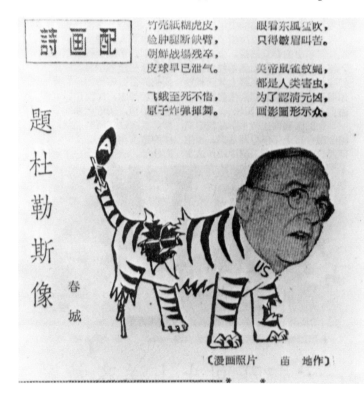

Tse-tung's effort to promote a uniquely Chinese solution to the problems of reorganizing and developing a traditional peasant society. Even the influence of the Soviet ally and the Russian pattern of revolution was challenged by Mao, who asserted to his comrades, "We cannot feed on meals cooked for us, or else defeat will be our lot. This point must be clearly explained to the Soviet comrades."[8]

Ironically, failures in the production of food engendered by the Great Leap Forward threatened the Party's dream of a rural population united through socialized production. The political pressures and haste with which the peasants had been organized into the People's Communes produced imbalances, and then, in the wake of successive natural disasters, failures in production. China plunged into three years of economic crisis; some elements of the population neared starvation. Not only did the difficulties created by the Great Leap shake the peasants' faith in socialism, it threatened the Party's foundation of popular support. In certain areas Commune cadres who had control over scanty grain reserves weathered the crisis without personal hardship while the common people suffered from malnutrition. Party leaders expressed fear of the hostility of the masses because of the cadres' oral indulgence:

> At present [early 1963], production and standards of living are not good and difficulties remain, even though some persons are demanding and extravagant with everything. The problem of excessive eating and drinking is also very severe and is also prominent among cadre members. As a result, a number of those among the masses have said that if we do not oppose these evil tendencies, it will be difficult to strengthen and expand the collective economy of the People's Communes. . . . This is especially so in regard to the problems of excessive eating and drinking, taking of special privileges and conveniences, and excessive spending and borrowing by the cadres.[9]

By the mid-1960s a reversion to pre-Great Leap rural organization and methods of agricultural production had enabled the Party to pass beyond the years of crisis and to restore grain production to the bumper level of 1958— albeit with an increase in *jen-k'ou* or "human mouths" (as the Chinese term "population") of upwards of 100 million. But while the production crisis was averted, the cultural and political tensions produced by Mao's effort to transform peasant China in one great leap increased as other Party leaders resisted the Chairman's policies. These tensions culminated in the Great Proletarian Cultural Revolution of 1966–69, another mass political upheaval in which Mao Tse-tung sought to remove from positions of power Party leaders opposed to his views. As the name Cultural Revolution implies, however, this struggle was also an attempt to reshape popular attitudes toward China's peasant past and her proletarian future. It was an effort to promote criticism of old customs and habits which Mao saw as impediments to the country's modernization. None of these cultural remnants was more basic than the eating rituals of old China which for so many centuries had served as the interpersonal cement of this agricultural society, binding together families and villages, ameliorating social conflict, and expressing a peasant culture's aspirations for security and social refinement. As an article in the Party's theoretical journal, *Red Flag,* emphasized, such old ways would have to pass if the workers' revolution were not to fall victim to China's remnant "class [cultural] enemy":

Is eating and drinking a mere trifle? No. Class struggle exists even at the tips of one's chopsticks. Under the conditions of proletarian dictatorship the class enemy will attack us not only with steel bullets but more frequently with sugar-coated bullets. They frequently make a breach in our mode of life first and take the faint-hearted captive in a bid to achieve their criminal aim of capitalist restoration. As the common saying goes, if you eat the things of others you will find it difficult to lift your hand against them. Eating and drinking with the class enemy . . . this shows that you and the enemy are sitting on the same bench and in the course of time you and the enemy will toe the same line and you will speak and act for the enemy and will be pulled into the water by the enemy.[10]

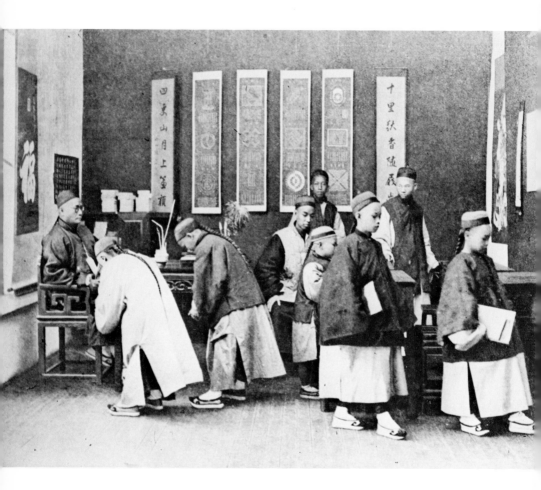

Words .3

言

While preoccupation with eating reflected the concern of China's people for security in a threatening world, respect for words and learning was an expression of the desire for high cultural achievement, a measure of deference to those in authority, and an indicator of political status. The power of the word in Chinese society can be seen as an elaboration of this strongly oral cultural pattern.

A Chinese child reared in traditional times was fed not only food, but social and political precepts as well. As an immature dependent, he was expected to take in the guidance of his elders just as he took in their material support. As one schoolteacher reared in Peking in the 1920s recalled of his childhood years:

> With father things had to be just so; there were rules for every-thing. At the dinner table we had to wait for the older people to

start eating first, we had to sit there at attention, and couldn't talk with our older brothers. . . . When father was speaking the children could not go on talking. Children were only allowed to listen to adults speaking because they didn't understand.[1]

A disciplined child in this tradition was considered one who would *t'ing hua,* "listen to talk"—the Chinese expression for "obedience."

For many growing children this relationship between words and authority was reinforced through formal Confucian education. A child whose family could afford thoughts of ambition learned at home that to be a mandarin, a cultured scholar-official, was the most prestigious and powerful career in his society. To win such status through competition in the imperial examinations would bring honor and wealth to his family and unquestioned respect for himself. In the classroom he learned that the power of the mandarins derived from their knowledge of words, their ability to quote the sayings of Confucius, to write essays in formal classical style, and to brush poems in elegant calligraphy. And for himself he saw that getting ahead in life was almost exclusively a matter of acquiring language skills. Control of words could bring control over one's destiny, and perhaps power over the lives of others as well.

Tsze-lu said, "The ruler of Wei has been waiting for you, in order for you to administer the government. What will you consider the first thing to be done?"

The Master replied, "What is necessary is to rectify names."

"If names be not correct, language is not in accordance with the truth of things. If language be not in accordance with the truth of things, affairs cannot be carried on to success. . . .

"Therefore a superior man considers it necessary that the names he uses may be spoken [appropriately], and also that what he speaks may be carried out [appropriately]. What the superior man requires is just that in his words there may be nothing incorrect."

—"The Analects" of Confucius[2]

This pattern of education created such a profound identification between literacy and the right to exercise political authority that Chinese leaders who rose to prominence through military conquest went to great lengths to "cultivate" their authority with the discipline of the brush, to justify their power with the skills of a scholar—and thus mask the sword with which power had been gained.

The majority of China's population in traditional times, however, never acquired the power of the word. Family and clan schools, or government academies, educated no more than a small percentage of what was largely an illiterate peasant population. Yet even those who never endured the rigors of a Confucian education accepted as part of the natural order of things the identification of words and power. The ritualistic origins of China's written language in fortune-telling through bone divination endured in the peasants' awe at finding a scrap of paper with a few brushed characters on it. Such paper would be saved rather than destroyed, reflecting respect for the authority of the written word and the power of the literate mandarins.

In less cultured ways, as well, those who exercised power in old China asserted their position through the word. One peasant recalled of service to his landlord:

> Any small mistake and [the landlord] blew up. I had to carry water through the gate [of his house]. There was a threshold with a sharp turn. If I spilled some water on the ground he cursed me for messing up the courtyard. Once I tore the horse's collar. He cursed me and my ancestors. I didn't dare answer back. I think that that was worse than the [bad] food and the filthy quarters—not being able to talk back. In those days the landlord's word was law. They had their way. When it was really hot and they said it was not, we dared not say it was hot; when it really was cold and they said it wasn't we dared not say it was cold. Whatever happened we had to listen to them.[3]

This was the tradition which China brought to the twentieth century—a social pattern of literary and political elitism coexistent with mass illiteracy and powerlessness. Despite the glories which Confucian government had brought to the empire in dynasties past, this tradition was to be violently rejected by many of those who eventually became the political leaders of the Chinese Communist movement. The military humiliations which China had suffered during the last days of the Ch'ing dynasty at the hands of Western nations made many young students at the turn of the century reject Confucianism for its demonstrated inability to cope with the challenges of a changed world. Ch'en Tu-hsiu, a classically trained scholar who was to found the Chinese Communist Party in 1921, attacked the imperial examination system as sterile and unsuited to the training of a new generation of officials who would solve China's problems. Ch'en and other intellectuals of what is now known as the "May Fourth" generation—after the anti-Western political demonstrations of May 4, 1919, in which the students of Peking protested the compromising of Chinese interests at the Versailles Peace Conference—sought to reshape their country's political tradition from elitism to mass participation. Their efforts began with rejection of the classical written language in favor of a written vernacular, along with promotion of mass literacy and popularized education.

The May Fourth generation was deeply influenced by the success of the Bolshevik revolution of 1917 in neighboring Russia. Instinctively sensing that the words of Marx and Lenin held answers to China's problems, students in the major cities formed "study groups" in an effort to extract from the ideology of the October Revolution new approaches to unifying their country and driving out foreign influence.

No member of the May Fourth generation was more sensitive to the importance of words in politics and of the need to transform the *uses* of language as a way of undermining the lingering influence of the Confucian tradition than Mao Tse-tung. Mao not only found in Marxism-Leninism concepts that could be used to revolutionize China, he also saw that China's "revolutionary" intellectuals continued to use their new ideology in traditional ways. They maintained a sense of elitism because of their unique skills with words, even as the political passivity of the rural population endured because of their entrapment in the thrall of illiteracy.

Two basic elements in the new style of political leadership which Mao Tse-tung developed over the years of struggle for power relate to the way that both the Communist Party and the Chinese people use words in politics. In the 1930s Mao attacked Party officials— "cadres," as they are termed in Chinese Communist parlance—who, like the mandarins of imperial times, were "book worshipers." Mao ridiculed local leaders who relied in their work solely on directives from the Party's central leadership, who "eat their fill and sit dozing in their offices all day long without ever moving a step and going out among the masses to investigate. Whenever they open their mouths, their platitudes make people sick."[5] Mao stressed the need for an activist style of leadership in which a Party official's right to issue orders to "the masses" grew not from knowledge of an abstract political doctrine, but from consciousness of social reality. As Mao phrased it, "No investigation [of political conditions], no right to speak."[6]

When I was thirteen I discovered a powerful argument of my own for debating with my father on his own ground, by quoting the Classics. My father's favorite accusations against me were of unfilial conduct and laziness. I quoted, in exchange, passages from the Classics saying that the elder must be kind and affectionate.
—Mao Tse-tung[4]

Other Party members, observed Mao, carried over the intellectual traditions of China's past in their use of Marxism, treating the doctrine as a new Confucianism to be expressed in the elegant style of the old imperial examination essays rather than a language of political agitation. "Some of our comrades love to write long articles with no substance, very much like 'the footbindings of a slattern, long as well as smelly.' Why must they write such long and empty articles? There can be only one explanation: They are determined the masses shall not read them."[7] Mao ridiculed others for their subjective and dogmatic use of the writings of Marx and Lenin: "We must tell [such people] openly, 'Your dogma is less useful than shit.' Dog shit can fertilize the fields . . . And dogmas? They can't fertilize the fields . . . Of what use are they? Comrades! You know the object of talk such as this is to ridicule those who regard Marxism-Leninism as dogma, to frighten and awaken them."[8]

In contrast, Mao heard in the bitter words of China's illiterate peasants the truth of hardship and injustice that the Party's revolution was intended to rectify. He sought to give a voice to the common people who, according to ancient custom, had to stand silent before

those in authority. The mass "speak bitterness" meetings which the Party organized during the struggles against Japanese invaders and the conservative Nationalist government gave a political voice to China's peasantry, enabling them to vent old grievances, raise their political consciousness, and thus gain popular support for the revolutionary cause.

Even if ten thousand schools of law and political science had been opened, could they have brought as much political education to the people, men and women, young and old, all the way into the remotest corners of the countryside, as the peasant associations have done in so short a time? I don't think they could. "Down with imperialism!" "Down with the warlords!" "Down with the corrupt officials!" "Down with the local tyrants and evil gentry!"—these political slogans have grown wings, they have found their way to the young, the middle-aged and the old, to the women and children in countless villages, they have penetrated into their minds and are on their lips.

Some of the peasants can also recite Dr. Sun Yat-sen's Testament. They pick out the terms "freedom," "equality," and "the Three People's Principles" and "unequal treaties" and apply them, if rather crudely, in their daily life. When somebody who looks like one of the gentry encounters a peasant and stands on his dignity, refusing to make way along a pathway, the peasant will say angrily, "Hey, you local tyrant, don't you know the Three People's Principles?" Formerly when the peasants from the vegetable farms on the outskirts of Changsha entered the city to sell their produce, they used to be pushed around by the police. Now they have found a weapon, which is none other than the Three People's Principles. When a policeman strikes or swears at a peasant selling vegetables, the peasant immediately answers back by invoking the Three People's Principles and that shuts the policeman up.

—Mao Tse-tung[9]

After the Communist victory in the civil war, the question for Mao became whether the Party would sustain the style of mass political participation developed during the revolutionary years, or whether the People's Republic of China would become a modern bureaucratic dynasty under the name of a socialist state. During the early 1950s the Chinese Communist Party, following the example of the Soviet Union, established political control by building a centralized party and state organization to rule China's vast population, manage the country's decentralized agricultural economy, and direct the growth of industry.

As a Marxist-Leninist, Mao was committed to the notion of "democratic-centralism" as a leadership concept; yet as he watched the party and state systems in operation, he saw more centralism than democracy. The Hungarian uprising of 1956 convinced him that without some form of public criticism directed at correcting bureaucratic abuses of power, the Chinese Communist Party would suffer the same fate of popular discontent and leadership strife that had befallen Stalin's Russia and the socialist countries of Eastern Europe.

In practice, Mao sought to establish a critical check on Party and state cadres by giving the Chinese people the power of the word, in the form of the opportunity to write public criticism of bureaucratic misuses of power. This was done through use of the *ta-tzu-pao,* or "big character poster," a type of wall newspaper long used in China as a way of publicizing governmental edicts. In the spring of 1957, with the Hungarian uprising still fresh in people's minds, Mao initiated a period of public debate and Party rectification under the slogan "Let a hundred flowers bloom, let a hundred schools of thought

Mao Tse-tung
and K'o Ch'ing-shih,
Mayor of Shanghai,
1957

contend." Relying on urban intellectuals and young students, the Chairman stimulated a public dialogue "to encourage argument and criticism among people holding different views, allowing freedom for both criticism and counter-criticism."[11]

Political work must take the mass line. It won't do to rely merely on the leaders alone. Can you handle so many things? Many good and bad deeds are not visible to you, and you can only see a part of them. It is therefore necessary to mobilize everybody to assume responsibility, speak out, give encouragement and make criticism. Everybody has a pair of eyes and a mouth. They should be allowed to use their eyes and mouths. It is democracy to let the masses handle their own affairs. In this connection there are two lines. One is to rely on individuals, and the other to mobilize the masses. Our politics is mass politics. Democratic politics must rely on the rule of all people, not a few people. It certainly is necessary to mobilize everybody to speak up. Since everybody has a mouth, he must bear two kinds of responsibility—to feed and to speak. He should speak out and take up the responsibility of fighting against bad deeds and bad styles of work.
—Mao Tse-tung[10]

"Chairman Mao holds meeting with representative personages of Shanghai's scientific, educational, literary, artistic, and industrial and commercial circles on July 7 [1957] at Shanghai's Sino-Soviet Friendship Building. The photograph shows Chairman Mao having intimate exchanges with them."

This public contention was not to be a liberal toleration of opposing political views, however. As a committed Marxist, Mao assumed the correctness of the Party's ideology, which he believed was China's only acceptable political doctrine. He asserted that Marxism would prove itself in a public debate: "Truth develops through its struggle against falsehood. This is how Marxism develops. Marxism develops in the struggle against bourgeois and petty-bourgeois ideology . . ."[12]

In practice, however, the mass criticism campaign of 1957 was not an exercise in creative Marxist political debate. Party members with mandarin notions that those in power should be beyond public attack resisted open criticism. At the same time, Western-influenced intellectuals and young students of the Communist era challenged the Party's right to monopolize political power. Mao's "hundred flowers" wilted in the heat of the critical voice of the students and intellectuals who questioned the "proletarian dictatorship," and in the resistance of Party cadres determined not to be subject to public ridicule.

The lesson which Mao drew from this experiment in mass criticism was not that public debate was wrong, but rather that "the people" could not be equated with the intellectuals—those who in traditional China had monopolized the power of the word. His problem was how to give expression to the views of the peasants and workers who comprised more than 85 per cent of China's population. Mao's answer came in 1958 in the context of the Great Leap Forward campaign—although the voice of China's rural masses was, in fact, to be but an echo of the Chairman's own conception of how to modernize Chinese society.

Apart from their other characteristics, the outstanding thing about China's 600 million people is that they are "poor and blank." This may seem a bad thing, but in reality it is a good thing. Poverty gives rise to the desire for change, the desire for action and the desire for revolution. On a blank sheet of paper free from any mark, the freshest and most beautiful characters can be written, the freshest and most beautiful pictures can be painted. The big-character poster is a very useful new weapon, which can be used in the cities and the rural areas, in factories, co-operatives, shops, government institutions, schools, army units and streets—in short, wherever the masses are to be found. It has already been widely used and should always be used. A poem written by Kung Tzu-chen of the Ching Dynasty reads:

Only in wind and thunder can the country show its vitality;
Alas, the ten thousand horses are all muted!
O Heaven! Bestir yourself, I beseech you,
And send down men of all the talents.

Big-character posters have dispelled the dullness in which "ten thousand horses are all muted."

—Mao Tse-tung[13]

Since 1955 Mao had been seeking a way to bring socialism to the traditionally fragmented and family-centered life of the Chinese peasants. The series of rural organizational reforms beginning with Mutual Aid Teams and running through the advanced Agricultural Producer's Co-operatives had brought about only marginal increases in agricultural production. At the same time, rapid industrialization in the cities had widened the economic and cultural gap between peasant China and the urban life of the workers and intellectuals.

In an effort to deal with these problems, Mao conceived of the rural areas organized into township or county-wide collectives which he called People's Communes. These were to be organizations of unified economic and political administration accounting for the activity of twenty thousand or more peasants, bringing light industry

人民日报

RENMIN RIBAO

1948年6月15日创刊
第 3686 号

毛主席

连声称赞人民公

新华社郑州11日电 毛泽东主席在8月6日到8日视察了河
农村。

毛主席在河南省视察了新乡县七里营人民公社的社办工业和
田；襄城县梁庄、薛元等农业社种植的烟叶和谷子；长葛县"
四"农业社的玉米田和商丘县进口乡中华农业社种植的红芋和
子。当毛主席在这些地方视察的时候，干部和群众都向毛主席热
欢呼，并且争着向毛主席报告农业社发展、巩固的情况和农业大
收的情况。毛主席在视察时同群众进行了亲切的谈话。陪同毛主
进行视察的有中共河南省委第一书记、河南省省长吴芝圃，中共
南省委书记处书记杨蔚屏、史向生以及有关地、县、乡的党委
责同志。

6日下午，毛主席到达新乡县七里营乡。这里的人民按照毛
席指示的道路，已经在全乡农业合作化的基础上建立了七里营人
公社。毛主席询问了这个公社的情况，并且参观了这个公社的托
所、"幸福院"、食堂、面粉加工厂、滚珠轴承厂，又到田间观
了棉花的生长情况。毛主席和在"幸福院"里过着晚年幸福生
的老年人握手，并且谈了话。在滚珠轴承厂里，毛主席详细地观
了用土法生产滚珠轴承的过程。他对这个小工厂在两天时间里就
产出五千多滚珠极为称赞。毛主席对于田间一望无际长得特别好
棉花达到特别赞许。毛主席走到正在棉花地里喷射杀虫药剂的女
们面前提议说："你们给我看看"，六个女社员兴高彩烈地给毛
席作了表演。毛主席走进了齐肩以上的棉花地，棉花的果枝上棉
成串，他连声称赞棉花长得好。毛主席从棉花地里走出来向社干

毛主席在河南视察农村时同少年 农民亲切地和棉花叶。
新华社记者 侯 波摄

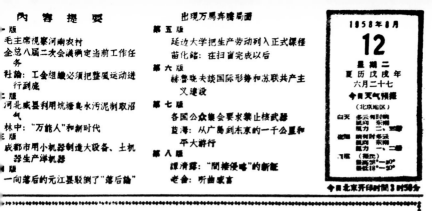

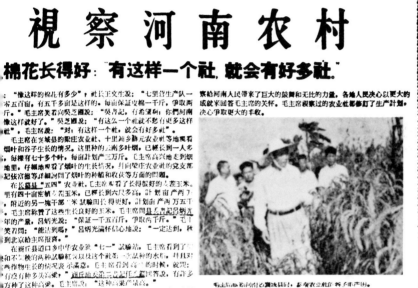

to the countryside in the form of fertilizer plants and back-yard steel smelters for making agricultural tools, and increasing the efficient use of China's most abundant natural resource—her population.

In an effort to promote these new organizations, which Mao assured the Party would accelerate the pace of "socialist construction" such that one day would equal twenty years of effort by bureaucratic means, the Chairman toured the countryside in the summer of 1958 in a widely publicized inspection of newly formed Communes. With the authoritative simplicity of a leader's word, Mao told his people, "It is best to form Communes." "If there is this kind of a Commune [in the province of Honan], then there can be many Communes."[14] Within a month fully one third of China's rural population had been organized into the new People's Communes.

According to the Party newspaper the *People's Daily,* the rapid formation of the Communes was an expression of the enthusiasm of the Chinese people for "building socialism." In fact, this reorganization of rural life was carried out in great haste and with political pressure applied by the Chinese Communist Party, which had been activated by its leader's word, ultimately bringing about three years of crisis in agricultural production. Mao himself came under criticism

from other Party leaders who felt that the Chairman—in traditional Chinese fashion—had overestimated the power of his own words. At a leadership meeting in the summer of 1959 Mao made a self-criticism before his colleagues:

> Diseases enter by the mouth and all disasters come through the tongue. I'm in great trouble today . . . I decided upon and promoted the target of 10,700,000 tons of steel, and as a result 90 million people were thrown into battle . . . Next, the People's Communes. I did not invent the People's Communes, but I promoted them. When I was in Shantung a correspondent asked me: "Are the People's Communes good?" I said, "Good"; and on the basis of this he published a report in a newspaper. From now on I must avoid reporters.[15]

Despite Mao's rhetorical recantation, the crisis of agricultural production generated by the Great Leap, which endured into the early 1960s, carried with it a crisis of confidence in Mao's leadership. This was manifest in veiled criticism of the Chairman which appeared in

the Party press, in the form of satires about dictatorial emperors in China's past, critical plays on historical themes, and ironic poems and newspaper columns. Some of the most pointed of these critical writings were the work of the editor of the *People's Daily*, Teng T'o, who published short commentaries on historical and social themes.

One of Teng T'o's columns, entitled "Talking Nonsense," criticized people who rejected scholarly research into social problems—an allusion to Mao's distrust of the intellectuals and his penchant for political activism. Another article, entitled "Great Empty Talk," ridiculed a neighbor who wrote high-sounding but meaningless poems with phrases such as "the East wind is our benefactor and the West wind our enemy"—a play on Mao's dictum of 1957 that the "East wind" (the "socialist camp") was prevailing over the "West wind" (the non-Communist world). In the vocabulary of Chinese politics there could be no more biting deprecation of the authority of a leader than the assertion that his words were nothing more than "great empty talk."[16]

Mao responded to this criticism in kind. If the Party bureaucracy would not respect his words, he would find others who would. At the same time that veiled criticism of the Chairman was appearing in the Party press, the People's Liberation Army began to promote the active study of Mao's word in the form of a little red book of quotations from his writings. China's Defense Minister, Lin Piao, began to be characterized in newspaper stories as "Chairman Mao's best student." The Army was gradually transformed into Mao's base of political support. The years 1961–65 thus saw the political tensions resulting from the crisis of the Great Leap Forward transformed into a conflict over authority and organizational power in which words became weapons of political combat. The Communist Party bureaucracy, rallying around Vice Chairman Liu Shao-ch'i, stressed classical Marxism-Leninism as the ideological basis of China's revolution, while Mao's supporters, backed by the People's Liberation Army, asserted that the "thought of Mao Tse-tung" was the highest development of Marxism-Leninism in the contemporary historical era.

The culmination of this leadership crisis was the Great Proletarian Cultural Revolution of 1966–69, the ultimate expression of the politics of the word, or, as Mao and his supporters characterized it, "verbal struggle" (*wen-tou*). The Chairman rallied the loyalty of China's masses around his little red book and set them

Ever since he assumed charge of the work of the Military Commission [in 1959], Comrade Lin Piao has called for holding high the great red banner of Mao Tse-tung's thought . . . On the other hand, Liu Shao-ch'i came out [in 1962] with his talks about "How to be a Good Communist," in which he shunned any mention of Mao Tse-tung's thought. Instead, for ulterior motives, he spoke lavishly of the need to become good pupils of the "creators" of Marxism-Leninism. . . .

Comrade Lin Piao pointed out as early as 1959: "Comrade Mao Tse-tung has comprehensively and creatively developed Marxism-Leninism. . . ." He further pointed out in 1960: "Mao Tse-tung's thought is the apex of Marxism-Leninism." Liu Shao-ch'i has openly opposed Comrade Lin Piao's view.[17]

Once Mao Tse-tung's thought is grasped by the broad masses, it becomes an inexhaustible source of strength and a spiritual atom bomb of infinite power.
—Lin Piao[18]

against his detractors in the Party leadership. The weapon used by students and workers in attacking Mao's enemies was the "big character poster," by means of which leaders who had resisted the Chairman's policies or authority were exposed to public criticism and repudiation. Mao's word triumphed. As his "best student," Lin Piao, asserted:

> Because Liu Shao-ch'i and his gang of counter-revolutionary revisionists had blocked Chairman Mao's instructions, the broad revolutionary masses could hardly hear Chairman Mao's voice directly. . . . The storm of the [Cultural Revolution] has made it possible for Mao Tse-tung's thought to reach the broad revolutionary masses directly. This is a great victory. The wide dissemination of Mao Tse-tung's thought in a big country with a population of 700 million is the most significant achievement of the Great Proletarian Cultural Revolution.[19]

While Mao was to win in the struggle against detractors of his political thought, in the complex world of China's politics he was not to have the last word, for those who acted as the instruments of "the thought of Mao Tse-tung" carried along with their ideological enthusiasm all the human frailties not found in the Chairman's idealized concepts of revolution. As the Cultural Revolution progressed, the student Red Guards, while criticizing Mao's enemies within the Party leadership, also began fighting among themselves for positions of local leadership. Rival factions claimed the role of the Chairman's exclusive spokesman and sought to suppress their opponents. As one of Mao's close supporters from Shanghai exclaimed in exasperation to a group of feuding students, "The reading of quotations [from Mao's little red book] has become nothing but a war of words."[20]

In these circumstances, Mao sought to restore political discipline among his supporters in a manner appropriate to a culture where the word is power: by having the feuding students submit to the rigors of political study. In the fall of 1968 workers and soldiers were organized into "Mao Tse-tung Thought Propaganda Teams" to lead students in the study of Mao's writings, thus transforming the use of the "thought of Mao Tse-tung" from a weapon of political attack to an instrument for reasserting order. No longer were students and workers permitted the freewheeling use of big character posters and the opportunity to criticize Party leaders which had characterized the "extensive democracy" of the Cultural Revolution's early days; "proletarian dictatorship" was reimposed through organized study of the leader's word.

While China's younger generation thus turned out to be less than model students of the Chairman's thought, Mao's ultimate loss was to come through a breakdown in the cohesiveness of the political leadership which weathered the storm of the Cultural Revolution. Resentment and distrust among various leaders produced in 1970 the purge of one of Mao's most intimate political spokesmen, Ch'en Po-ta, and in the following year it led to the political undoing of the

man who had propagated Mao's word in the Cultural Revolution, Lin Piao. In the summer of 1971, Lin—apparently under attack by other leaders who resented his actions during the Cultural Revolution, and who opposed him for the power he had accumulated in the Army—planned what proved to be an unsuccessful coup against Mao and other leaders. He further discredited himself as a traitor by fleeing China toward the Soviet Union when his plotting was discovered, only to die when his plane crashed in Mongolia.

With Lin Piao's sudden and unsettling demise vanished the aura of infallibility and authority surrounding Mao's word, which Lin had used as the vehicle of his rise to power. Lin Piao was denounced in the Chinese press as a "political swindler" who had hoodwinked the masses through the use of "elegant words" and "idealistic aphorisms," and by "playing empty word games" with Mao's political thought.[21] By the summer of 1972 the Party press, in an effort to sustain ideological unity amid political confusion, emphasized the need for cadres to study the works of Marx, Engels, Lenin, and Stalin—with hardly a reference to Mao's writings.

Thus Mao's word, rather than being an expression of timeless truth, has been both victor and victim in the vagaries of Party political conflict. Yet Mao Tse-tung's influence on the Chinese revolution lies not so much in the fate of his writings as in the new *uses* of words which he has promoted. Mass literary campaigns, group criticism meetings, and popular criticism of those in authority through the big character posters are the elements of a fundamental change in China's political tradition, if only these new expressions of the power of the word are sustained by Mao's successors and new generations of China's millions.

Emulation .4

模範

A Chinese child practicing characters in his lesson book learned more than just language; he was being taught that sources of authority are models to be copied. The aura of authority that was vested in words by virtue of the power of the scholar-officials gave language learning the quality of a lesson in leadership: those in positions of authority were to be studied and emulated.

The notion of leadership as presenting a model to follow pervades China's social institutions. Within the family a child was taught to follow uncritically the behavior of his father and elder brothers.

His ancestors were presented to him as models of virtue. By emulating them he would both honor their memory and bring added virtue to future generations.

In school the teacher was viewed by his students not just as a source of knowledge, but as a model figure from whom to learn moral behavior. The Confucian classics instructed a teacher to "be an exemplar by your actions" (*yi-shen tso-tse*), and in teaching his pupils he was to present China's great cultural heritage, its classical literature and philosophy, not through critical interpretation but as moral standards to be memorized without question. Even in the study of poetry, painting, and sculpture the established forms of past masters were presented as models to be copied. Creativity in the Confucian tradition did not mean formulating new ideas or artistic forms, but giving renewed expression to the exemplary achievements of the past. Copying was viewed not as plagiarism but as seeking to attain past standards of greatness, while innovation smacked of disrespect for those in authority, or even of rebelliousness.

The emulation concept of leadership permeated the highest source of authority in the imperial tradition. Confucian political thinking characterized the emperor as a model for all society. If his personal behavior were correct, asserted the classical literature, then the empire would be ordered and at peace, while immoral behavior on his part would bring social turmoil and rebellion. This was described as follows in "The Great Learning":

> Let the ruler discharge his duties to his elder and younger brothers, and then he may teach the people of the state.

> In the *Book of Poetry* it is said, "In his deportment there is nothing wrong; he rectifies all the people of the state." Yes; when the ruler, as a father, a son, and a brother, is a model, then the people imitate him.[1]

China's traditional pattern of international relations, known as the "tribute system," was also based on the emulation concept of authority. The emperor viewed China, not as one state among equals, but as a model civilization for less cultured peoples to emulate. The Chinese term for "China" is *Chung-kuo,* the "Middle Kingdom," the center of culture and social organization. In traditional times foreigners were permitted into the country only on the understanding that they came to pay respect to the emperor as the highest source of authority in the civilized world. This deference was expressed by performing the ritual *kow-tow* (*k'o-t'ou*), or three kneelings and nine knockings

of the head, before the emperor, and by presenting gifts of appreciation for the privilege of access to the imperial presence. In abiding
by this act of submission, the "barbarian" visitor reaffirmed the
power of the emperor as a model of virtue in the eyes of the Chinese
people. If a stranger would pay the emperor such respect, could his
Chinese subjects have any doubts about imperial authority?

Such doubts did result, however, from the unwillingness in modern
times of militarily powerful foreigners to show deference to the emperor. The Western nations which forced themselves upon China in
the nineteenth century, as the Mongols and Manchus had done in

The Empress Dowager, Tzu Hsi, surrounded by ladies of the foreign diplomatic corps who call on her in Peking in 1903. On her left, holding her hand, is Sarah Conger, wife of the American minister to the Ch'ing Court

earlier times, helped to destroy the political "face" of imperial authority. The British, French, Russians, Japanese, and Americans who sought trade and access to China for their missionaries and educators, who demanded that the Ch'ing emperor receive them in Peking as political equals, undermined the authority of the Manchu imperial house in the eyes of its Chinese subjects, thus hastening the collapse of the last Confucian dynasty and accelerating the trend toward social and political revolution.

The concept of authority as a model to be emulated is inherently a conservative doctrine, for one is bound by past experience and established forms as guides to behavior. The problem confronting China's young revolutionaries in the early years of this century was how to overcome the weight of their country's cultural inheritance, which not only emphasized the "good old days" of a glorious Confucian past, but also embodied an intellectual tradition which discouraged innovation and self-assertiveness. The manner in which this problem was solved accorded with China's cultural pattern, but it also embodied a contradiction which has shaped political controversies of more recent days. In searching for solutions to their country's future, some members of the "May Fourth" students generation saw in Russia's Bolshevik revolution a model experience worthy of emulation. Lenin's party appeared to have solved the very problems of political weakness, vulnerability to foreign intervention, and economic backwardness that plagued their own society. Thus, the founding of the Chinese Communist Party in 1921 was stimulated by the apparently successful Marxist-Leninist revolution in neighboring Russia.

The earnest and uncritical spirit with which these young Chinese revolutionaries sought to emulate the Soviet example bespoke their need for a model to follow; yet their rigid adherence to this alien experience led to disastrous tactical mistakes as they sought to re-create an urban, working-class revolution in what was still a peasant society. The failures of urban uprisings in Nanchang and Canton in 1927 forced the Party leadership to develop political and military tactics appropriate to China's circumstances. The building of a peasant army based in remote provincial border areas, the promotion

THE REVOLUTIONARY BASE—YENAN

of social revolution through land reform, and Party leadership of a protracted national struggle against a foreign invader constituted a new international model of revolution that in the 1930s came to be associated with Communist Party Chairman Mao Tse-tung and his military cohort Chu Teh. In tribute to these men and their cause,

Agnes Smedley in Yenan, 1937   Chu Teh in Yenan, 1937

Americans like Agnes Smedley and William Hinton journied to the Communists' wartime capital of Yenan and other areas which had been "liberated" by the Party, thus reaffirming for the Chinese the justness of their struggle through the foreigners' desire to emulate them by personal involvement.

William Hinton
in Long Bow Village,
Shansi Province, 1947

Mao Tse-tung

In the history of Chinese Communism there has been a constant and delicate balance between the inspiration and sense of identity derived from the Party's association with the Soviet Union and the need to adapt "the universal truths of Marxism-Leninism" to the particular circumstances of Chinese society. On the eve of the founding of the People's Republic in 1949, Mao Tse-tung stressed that the new China would "lean to one side" in its international relations; that is, the country would orient itself toward the Soviet Union in the process of national reconstruction. "The Communist Party of the Soviet Union is our best teacher and we must learn from it," said Mao.[2]

At about the same time, however, Mao's cohort Liu Shao-ch'i asserted to a Party-convened international trade union conference in Peking that "the path taken by the Chinese people in defeating imperialism and its lackeys and in founding the People's Republic of China is the path that should be taken by the peoples of various colonial and semi-colonial countries in their fight for national independence and people's democracy."[3] This tension between the Chinese Communists' orientation toward the Soviet Union and their claim to have developed a unique model of revolution was sufficiently great that—as Mao Tse-tung himself was to reveal—Josef Stalin distrusted Mao as an assertive nationalist and was reluctant to ally the Soviet Union with the new Chinese Communist state.[4]

This balance between commitment to the Soviet precedent of revolution and development of a Chinese model has also been at the center of policy conflict within the leadership of the Chinese Communist Party. During the early 1950s, as the Party acquired experience in the process of "socialist transformation" of China's economy and social system, divergences in judgment developed within the leadership about the best way to modernize the country. These policy differences came to be expressed in terms of reference to Soviet or Maoist models of revolution.

In mid-1955 Mao Tse-tung, in a major policy speech on problems of agricultural development, expressed his exasperation with "com-

---

We must emphasize internationalism and study the strong points of the Soviet Union and other foreign countries. This is one principle. But in studying there are two approaches: one is to be exclusively imitative; the other is [to study] with a spirit of independence and creativity. In studying we must combine a sense of independence and creativity, while to adopt the system and regulations of the Soviet Union rigidly is to contravene the spirit of independence and creativity. . . . After our entire country was liberated (1950 to 1956), dogmatism appeared in our economic work and cultural and educational work. . . . This also was the case in public health work. For three years they warned me not to eat chicken eggs or to drink chicken soup because the Soviet Union had an article which said you shouldn't eat chicken eggs or chicken soup. But later they said I could eat them. No matter whether the Soviet articles were accurate or not, Chinese people obeyed them, implemented them. In everything, the Soviet Union was Number One.

—Mao Tse-tung[5]

---

rades who use the Soviet experience as a cover for their idea of moving at a snail's pace" in the collectivization of agriculture.[6] Mao's personal judgment was that the Soviet pattern of economic construction, in which heavy industry received the greatest share of capital investment and human talent, was inappropriate to the needs of developing a peasant society. He stressed the importance of keeping increases in agricultural production and the improvement of rural life in step with the programs of industrialization and urban development. Rather than seeing heavy industry as a "leading factor" which, once developed, would pull along production in the rural areas, Mao felt that the economy must "walk on two legs" by developing agriculture in step with the industrial sector.

To implement this policy, Mao began to develop a model of collectivized agriculture drawn from the "advanced experience" of China's most successful Agricultural Producers' Co-operatives. This model experience was publicized for emulation by Party cadres in early 1956 in a book of examples of agricultural collectivization entitled *Socialist Upsurge in China's Countryside*. In a widely circulated "Preface" to the volume, which was edited by the Chairman himself, Mao asserted that in large-scale collective farms "the broad masses for the first time have clearly seen their future."[8]

While lower-level Party cadres pressed the peasantry to adopt Mao's evolving vision of socialized agriculture, Party leaders opposed to his line continued to stress the primary importance of industrialization. These men were able to bring to a temporary halt the formation of collective farms in mid-1956, claiming the need to gradually accustom the rural population to the new organizations. In the summer of the following year, however, continuing shortfalls in agricultural production enabled Mao to reassert with greater force the need for a *Chinese* solution to the problems of the country's economic modernization.

The most developed form of Mao Tse-tung's model of collectivized agricultural production grew from leadership debates and experimentation in collectivized management during the winter and spring of 1957–58. Following a Party Congress which reasserted the leading role of "the thought of Mao Tse-tung" in determining national policy, Mao and his supporters promoted the concept of the People's Commune as an integral and self-reliant organization of production, administration, and national defense designed to make the most effective use of China's great labor force. The Commune—as with the contemporary national agricultural model at Tachai, in Shansi Province—was presented to the Chinese people as a model social unit which would rapidly increase agricultural production and improve the quality of life. As Mao's close comrade Ch'en Po-ta asserted, "Under the leadership of this great red flag [of the People's Commune concept], the Chinese people, in the not-distant future,

The Communist Party's propaganda policy . . . should be, "Draw the bow without shooting, just indicate the motions." It is for the peasants themselves to cast aside the idols [of traditional rural life] . . . it is wrong for anybody else to do it for them.
—Mao Tse-tung[7]

Tachai People's Commune, Shansi Province

农业学大寨

"In agriculture learn from Tachai"

will steadily and victoriously advance to the great Communist society."⁹

In practice, however, Mao's model of rural development did not produce the millennium. The economic hardships of 1959–61, described above, sharpened disputes and rivalry within the Party leadership. In part, these political tensions took the form of contending factions promoting different model figures for the people to emulate. Mao's supporters in the People's Liberation Army promoted the young martyr Lei Feng as a model for Chinese youth to follow. Lei was an army transportation officer whose outstanding qualities were his exemplary behavior as a student of Mao's political thought

and his love for the Chairman. Lei's personal fate was
death in a truck accident, yet he lived on as a symbol of
loyalty to Mao for China's youth to study.

Mao's opponents within the Party and the Army responded by promoting alternative model individuals and
organizational experiences for the Chinese people to follow. One such figure was Huang Chi-kuang, a hero of
the Korean War, whose short life and martyr's death
were recorded as a model for children—but without
mention of his inspiration by "the thought of Mao Tse-
tung." Another was Chao Yu-lu, a county Party secretary
whose achievements were guided by Marxism-Leninism
rather than by the Chairman's writings.[10]

毛主席是我们心中的红太阳

This struggle of emulation escalated to the point where Mao Tse-tung himself was described to the people of China and to the world as an outstanding genius of the present historical epoch who had developed Marxism-Leninism to a new stage, the ultimate model of a revolutionary for Chinese students and progressive peoples around the world to emulate.

> Comrade Mao Tse-tung is the greatest Marxist-Leninist of our era. He has inherited, defended and developed Marxism-Leninism with genius, creatively and comprehensively, and has brought it to a higher and completely new stage.
>
> —Lin Piao[11]

In the ensuing turmoil of the Cultural Revolution, however, as Mao sought to remove from power Party leaders opposed to his model of revolution, China's student Red Guards proved themselves to be something less than exemplars of the Chairman's political thought.

Factional struggles fragmented the student movement and produced loss of life and property unrelated to Mao's attack on "revisionist" Party leaders. Even the man who had been the major proponent of "the thought of Mao Tse-tung," Lin Piao, was to fall from power, apparently the loser in a struggle for leadership in which his role as sponsor of the Cultural Revolution's most disruptive forces left him with few political supporters.

As stated above, Lin Piao's demise, in September 1971, brought criticism of his characterization of Mao as a historical genius. The Chairman, in more humble terms, told his American friend Edgar Snow, in a moment of self-criticism for the personality cult which had grown up around him during the Cultural Revolution, that he only wished to be remembered by future generations as a great teacher.[12] In the Chinese tradition, however, a teacher has long been considered a model to be emulated by his students, a source of authority rather than an independent intellect who just stimulates his students on to their own achievements. Thus Mao, even as a teacher of revolution, is likely to remain a powerful model figure who will long be held up for emulation by China's millions, a symbol of political legitimacy to be used by successive generations of Party leaders.

孤立

Complementing the Chinese view of their leaders as models to be emulated is the use of "negative models" to control social deviance. While a family head, teacher, or political figure stood above the social collective as a guide to be followed, those in positions of authority sought to ensure social discipline by bringing group pressure to bear on dependents who did not follow their lead. And in a society which taught its children to find security and social identity through group interdependence, the fear of being isolated from group respect and material support, of being shamed before family or exposed to ridicule before village neighbors, constituted a powerful form of social control.

Chinese remember that the punishments of childhood sensitized them to their "face" before family and friends. "For big mistakes we would have to kneel before the family group after dinner and be scolded," a teacher recalled of his youth in a well-to-do Peking family.[1] Failure to perform well in school might be met with a parental demand that the child, as punishment, "sit beside the dinner table and watch everyone else eat."[2] In the classroom, improper behavior could lead to the offending student being made to stand in shame before ridiculing classmates.[3]

The sanctions of the adult world similarly played on fears of shame and isolation which were the legacy of childhood. In traditional China there was the ritual of "cursing the street," in which the aggrieved party to a dispute would air his complaint loudly in public to call attention to the person who had done him wrong, thus bringing

shame or disrepute on the offending individual.[4] More serious public offenders—hoodlums or thieves—would suffer the humiliation of the cangue, or penal collar, which exposed their faces to public shame. And for the most serious offenses of murder or political opposition there was the ultimate "loss of face" of decapitation and having one's severed head exposed in public as a warning to others.

As China's political life began to be transformed in the early twentieth century from an exclusive affair of the Confucian elite to the realm of mass popular involvement, the forms of social control familiar to China's "masses" shaped the style of revolutionary politics. In the 1920s, as Mao Tse-tung began his efforts to gain peasant support for the Communist Party's social revolution, Mao wrote of the power of public shaming as a way to discredit the "face" of China's conservative rural elite. He marveled at the political impact which the Peasant Associations gained by "crowning the landlords and parading them through the villages":

This sort of thing is very common. A tall paper-hat is stuck on the head of one of the local tyrants or evil gentry, bearing the words "Local tyrant so-and-so" or "So-and-so of the evil gentry." He is led by a rope and escorted with big crowds in front and behind. Sometimes brass gongs are beaten and flags waved to attract people's attention. This form of punishment more than any other makes the local tyrants and evil gentry tremble. Anyone who has once been crowned with a tall paper-hat loses face altogether and can never again hold up his head. Hence many of the rich prefer being fined to wearing the tall hat. But wear it they must if the peasants insist. One ingenious township Peasant Association arrested an obnoxious member of the gentry and announced that he was to be crowned that very day. The man turned blue with fear. Then the association decided not to crown him that day. They argued that if he were crowned right away, he would become case-hardened and no longer afraid, and that it would be better to let him go home and crown him some other day. Not knowing when he would be crowned, the man was in daily suspense, unable to sit down or sleep at ease.[5]

Mao found that by thus isolating enemies of the revolution, China's peasants gained confidence in their role as the main force of a mass revolutionary movement.

Mao knew well, however, of the danger of losing popular support which was inherent in pressing a conservative peasantry to initiate radical social change. During the late 1920s, when the Communist Party had been driven into the rural wilds of Kiangsi Province by Chiang Kai-shek's armies, Mao wrote with deep concern of the movement's loss of peasant backing:

Wherever the Red Army goes, the masses are cold and aloof, and only after our propaganda do they slowly move into action. Whatever enemy units we face there are hardly any cases of mutiny or desertion to our side and we have to fight it out. . . . We have an acute sense of our isolation which we keep hoping will end.[6]

From Mao's sensitivity to political isolation grew his never-ending exhortation to the Party that it must not "cut itself off from the masses" through actions or policies which would alienate popular support.

Gaining peasant backing for the Party meant, in part, organizing the rural population for united action against those who held power in the countryside:

. . . on the strength of their extensive organization the peasants have gone into action and within four months they have brought about a great revolution in the countryside, a revolution without parallel in history. . . . This astonishing and accelerating rate of expansion explains why the local tyrants, evil gentry and corrupt officials have been isolated.[7]

Fully overturning the forces of traditional village life, however, required humiliating in the eyes of the peasantry the landlords and those who had directly supported their rule. Thus the "face-destroying" parade of duncecapped landlords used in the 1920s was transformed into the more violent struggle of the civil war and land reform periods, in which Party cadres urged the peasants to strike, and sometimes kill, their former rulers who now stood isolated before the powerful People's Liberation Army.

Organized efforts to isolate and humiliate Party enemies before the masses were to find varied use in the days after the Liberation of 1949. In order to discredit those who had supported the Nationalist government, sports stadiums were turned over to mass public trials, where "evil elements," spies, landlords, and former Nationalist officials were dragged out for isolated exposure before the masses.

In 1958, Mao Tse-tung sought to conclude the unresolved civil war with the Nationalists through a military confrontation which would isolate the Nationalist-held offshore islands of Quemoy and Matsu. Chinese Communist propaganda of this period reveals the potency in Chinese eyes of isolation and public humiliation as ways of dealing with Party enemies. The well-known intellectual Kuo Mo-jo wrote a poem telling his countrymen that they were supported by the world's people in their struggle against "U.S. Imperialism," which would perish in shame before the "pointing fingers" of an indignant world population:

> Our brothers of the Soviet Union
> and Eastern Europe
> Are all fighters for peace.
> Asia, Africa and Latin America
> Are all our comrades, opposing war.
> Have you [Americans] not heard that
> the man at whom all fingers point
> Perishes, even though he has no sickness?
> How much more the raving maniac
> Who dares provoke the wrath of all
> mankind![8]

Such tactics, while ineffective in China's international relations, were to prove viable for Mao Tse-tung in confronting opponents within the Party who resisted his many political initiatives of the late 1950s. During the Cultural Revolution of 1966–1969 Mao discredited Party officials who had opposed his policies by having them dragged out in isolated humiliation before Army men and student Red Guards. Even the wife of Mao's long-time cohort Liu Shao-ch'i, Wang Kuang-mei, was decked out in a dowdy Western-style dress and Ping-pong ball necklace and "struggled" by the Red Guards for her "bourgeois" behavior while on a diplomatic tour of Indonesia in 1962.[9]

Mao was to find, however, that the traditional forms of group control which had become a part of Party rule still inhibited many of the masses from standing above the crowd to criticize Party "revisionists." Even Party cadres resisted breaking organizational discipline to attack their "counterrevolutionary" superiors. In October 1966 the *People's Daily* sought to discredit this conservative tendency by glorifying the revolutionary writer Lu Hsun, who, in the May Fourth era, had dared to stand above the crowd and criticize China's ancient ways and the officials who sustained feudal tradition. "Fierce-

When a wrong [political] tendency surges toward us like a rising tide, we must not fear isolation and must dare to go against the tide and brave it through. Chairman Mao states: "Going against the tide is a Marxist-Leninist principle."
—Chou En-lai, "Report to the Tenth National Congress of the Communist Party of China" (1973)

browed, I coolly defy a thousand pointing fingers," Mao's hero Lu Hsun had written[10]; and in 1966, China's younger generation, with guidance from the Party Chairman, rose to criticize their elders who were still burdened with the "four olds" of China's traditional culture, ideas, customs, and habits.

Despite Mao's encouragement of Party cadres and students to stand out above the crowd and criticize the wrongdoings of those in authority, and his attempt to give ideological legitimacy to the principle of "going against the tide" of group opinion, the collectivist orientation of China's cultural pattern remains a strong inhibition on individualistic and self-assertive behavior. Not only has Mao himself encouraged isolation forms of punishment and group pressures to control individual deviance, but there has also been a clear pattern in recent years indicating that those leaders who stood out above the collective or asserted themselves in criticism of the Chairman's policies—such as P'eng Teh-huai, Liu Shao-ch'i, and Lin Piao—did not long survive the play of leadership politics. To be an outstanding leader worthy of emulation is its own form of isolation, and it may be significant that the only model heroes who have endured in the imagery of Chinese Communism, most notably Lu Hsun and Lei Feng, are deceased. Thus it remains uncertain whether the personal independence and criticality of spirit essential to innovation and mass criticism of the errors or misdeeds of those in authority will grow in a society which continues to subordinate the individual to collective needs.

Swimming .6

游泳

The symbols of China's cultural and political revolution have been formed, in dialectical fashion, as a reaction against the values and traditions of the old society. There is no image of the revolution which more forcefully combines rejection of Confucianism with the struggle to create a new social order than that of swimming. The act with which Mao Tse-tung initiated his Cultural Revolution in 1966 draws its significance from a cultural tradition which discouraged physical and individual assertiveness, and sums up Mao's lifelong career of rebellion against established authority.

The subordination of individual to family purposes in Confucian society was expressed, in part, through great physical reserve. A growing (male) child's bodily health was seen as the basis of parental security in old age, the guarantor of family continuity in subsequent generations. Any physical assertiveness on the part of a growing child which might endanger his health was strongly discouraged. Chinese reared in traditional times recall being thrashed by their parents when they engaged in such adolescent horseplay as tree climbing or swimming with friends.

This attitude found formal expression in the life style of China's traditional social elite: in the aloofness from manual labor, the measured gait, and the long fingernails of the mandarins. The Confucian classics stressed to children of the educated elite that protection of one's body was the foundation of moral virtue. As the *Classic of Filial Piety* instructed: "Our bodies—to every hair and bit of skin—are received from our parents, and we must not presume to injure or wound them; this is the beginning of filial piety."[1]

This association of physical inhibition with subordination to those in authority had added meaning for Chinese during the Ch'ing dynasty, when the long hair plait or queue was worn by Han (or native) Chinese as a sign of submission to the rule of the alien Manchus.

How would an individual reared in this tradition express opposition to the harshness of filial subordination to parental authority, to labor for the family collective that might not be rewarded with a measure of attention to individual concerns, or to the fear of being committed to an arranged marriage that conformed to family interests at the expense of personal desires? Some answers to these questions, as well as the problems themselves, can be found in the personal experience of Mao Tse-tung.

An unusually assertive young Mao recalled that his father "was a severe taskmaster. He hated to see me idle, and if there were no [account] books to be kept he put me to work at farm tasks. He was a hot-tempered man and frequently beat both me and my brothers. He gave us no money whatever, and the most meagre food."[2] Mao's memories of his mother, in contrast, were of "a kind woman, generous and sympathetic." Yet, following the cultural norm, she would not openly oppose the harshness of her husband. "My mother advocated a policy of indirect attack. She criticized any overt display of emotion and attempts at open rebellion against the [family] Ruling Power. She said it was not the Chinese way."[3] Reflecting the habit of generations of Chinese women to turn aggression against the self—for example, by resorting to suicide by drowning in a river or well as the only alternative to an intolerable arranged marriage—Mao's mother instructed him to "eat his bitterness" and avoid open confrontations with paternal authority.

By constitution, however, Mao was too assertive to hold in his frustrations. His tolerance of paternal harshness ended when his father tried to humiliate him before a group of family friends:

> When I was about thirteen my father invited many guests to his home, and while they were present a dispute arose between the two of us. My father denounced me before the whole group, calling me lazy and useless. This infuriated me. I cursed him and left the house.[4]

Mao's youthful response combined an innate forcefulness of character with his mother's strategy of "indirect attack":

> My father pursued me, cursing at the same time that he commanded me to come back. I reached the edge of a pond and threatened to jump in if he came any nearer. In this situation demands and counter-demands were presented for a cessation of the "Civil War." My father insisted that I apologize and k'o-t'ou as a sign of submission. I agreed to give a one-knee k'o-t'ou if he would promise not to beat me. Thus the war ended, and from it I learned that when I defended my rights by open rebellion my father relented, but when I remained meek and submissive he only cursed and beat me the more.[5]

Mao Tse-tung's family home at Shaoshan, Hunan Province

Thus, the pond before the family house at Shaoshan became for Mao Tse-tung a personal symbol of opposition to authority. Before long, however, Mao transformed the threat of self-destruction through drowning by which he had challenged his father into more positive efforts to break out of the bonds of filial subordination. Rather than drown, Mao taught himself to swim. He recounted to Edgar Snow that he became an ardent physical culturist:

In the winter [school] holidays we tramped through the fields, up and down mountains, along city walls, and across the streams and rivers. If it rained we took off our shirts and called it a rain bath. When the sun was hot we also doffed shirts and called it a sun bath. In the spring winds we shouted that this was a new sport called "wind bathing." We slept in the open when frost was already falling, and even in November swam in the cold rivers. All this went on under the title of "body training."[6]

The relation of Mao's physical assertiveness to his eventual political rebellion was suggested when he observed that the bodily endurance he acquired in such activity helped him "to build the physique I was to need so badly later in my many marches back and forth across South China and on the Long March from Kiangsi to the North West."[7]

The tradition-breaking impact of such physical activity found varied expression in the social ferment of China in the first years of this century. A strong-willed Chu Teh, who was to join Mao in founding the Red Army, scandalized his family by becoming a teacher of physical education.[8] And the intensifying political protest of Han Chinese against the weakened Ch'ing dynasty was manifest in physical assaults against that most personal symbol of subordination to the Manchus, the queue. Mao Tse-tung recalled that the students in his high school "demonstrated their anti-Manchu sentiments by a rebellion against the pigtail. One friend and I clipped off our pigtails, but the others, who had promised to do so, afterward failed to keep their word. My friend and I therefore assaulted them in secret and forcibly removed their queues, a total of more than ten falling victim to our shears." One student resisted, holding that "the body, skin, hair, and nails are heritages from one's parents and must not be destroyed, quoting the Classics to clinch his argument. But I myself and the anti-pigtailers developed a countertheory on an anti-Manchu political basis, and thoroughly silenced him."[9] The inviolability of the body which was the basis of filial piety thus came under attack as the last imperial Confucian dynasty neared its final days.

A more explicit political analysis of the relationship between China's weakness as a nation and the Confucian tradition of physical reserve was developed by Mao Tse-tung in his first major political tract, "A Study of Physical Education." Writing in 1917 in the influential radical periodical *New Youth,* Mao lamented, "Our nation is wanting in strength. The military spirit has not been encouraged. The physical condition of the population deteriorates daily. This is an extremely disturbing phenomenon."[10] Mao drew on his own teen-age habit of taking ice-water baths as a way of developing physical stamina and will-power in the search for a solution to China's political demoralization:

> Physical education not only harmonizes the emotions, it also strengthens one's will. . . . Such aspects of the martial spirit as courage, dauntlessness, audacity, and perseverence are all matters of will. Let me explain this with an example. If we wash our feet in ice water we will develop courage and dauntlessness as well as audacity. In general, any form of exercise, if pursued continuously, will help train us in perseverance.[11]

From such views evolved Mao's leadership style, which stressed political discipline and daring, struggle with enemies, and reliance on physical labor as a way of heightening political consciousness. From Mao's youthful assertiveness grew a political-military strategy which characterized the Red Army as "fish" swimming among the people, and a defense doctrine which stressed "drowning enemies in the ocean of people's war."[12]

The Communist Party's attainment of power in 1949 reflected in no small measure the forceful leadership and personal style of Mao Tse-tung. Yet the enormous tasks which the Party faced in consolidating its rule and rebuilding China's war-shattered economy forced upon it a unity of leadership in which Mao seems to have been, at most, first among equals. Making collective decisions about how to modernize the country, the Party leadership embarked on a course of economic reconstruction which concentrated on development of heavy industry, urbanization, and creation of a conventional military machine—policies which were directed by a Party and state bureaucracy structured on the model of Stalin's Russia.

By the early 1950s, however, this approach to China's development became an issue of debate within the Party leadership. In the face of failures in agricultural production, Mao began to consider new approaches to social and economic change. These brought him into opposition with the Soviet precedent of economic development, as well as with a rival for leadership of the Chinese Communist Party. Mao's rival was Kao Kang, leader of the Party's Manchurian bureau and Chairman of the powerful State Planning Commission. Kao was not only a leading spokesman for the Soviet model of development but also a man of talent and ambition whose growing power seems to have stirred Mao into challenging the "conventional wisdom" of Russian economic practices.

Mao moved successfully in 1953 and 1954 to oust Kao Kang from positions of leadership, and in mid-1955 he pressed the Party to mobilize China's peasants in an effort to speed the pace of social and economic development in the rural areas. The Party Chairman was attempting to turn the techniques of mass mobilization and political struggle, which had been so successful in the War of Resistance against Japan and the Civil War, to the tasks of social and economic construction in the postrevolutionary era.

The objections of some other Party leaders to Mao's development policies did not end with the purging of Kao Kang, however. When the Soviet leader Nikita Khrushchev attacked Stalin's "cult of personality" at the Twentieth Congress of the Soviet Communist Party in February 1956, these leaders in the Chinese Party acquired the political leverage to restrict Mao's influence within the bounds of collective Party leadership. They tried to forestall a Maoist "cult of personality," and limit the Party Chairman's application of "revolutionary" policies which they felt were inappropriate to an era of peaceful economic development.

As Mao watched his efforts to speed up the pace of China's national development being thwarted by cautious comrades, he expressed his frustration in two swims across the Yangtze in the late spring of 1956. A poem Mao brushed in memory of this exploit describes his impatient "pacing" outside the center of political influence:

Swimming across the
    ten-thousand-li long Yangtze
Deep I gaze my fill
    into far Chu skies;
Heedless of boisterous winds
    and buffeting waves,
Better this seemed than leisurely
    pacing home courtyards:
Today I have indeed
    obtained my release.[13]

力
争
上
游

The Party Chairman was not to be restricted for long, however. By 1958 continuing stagnation in the rural economy and criticism of the Party by "bourgeois" urban intellectuals gave Mao grounds for convincing other leaders that with active Party guidance China's peasants could bring about a "Great Leap Forward" in economic development.

Mao's personal role in formulating the Great Leap initiative was evident in one of the slogans of the campaign: "Strive for the upper reaches of the river."[14] As the rural population was organized into the People's Communes for a collective assault on the country's economic backwardness, Mao met with members of the Wuhan municipal swimming team while on a tour of communes in the Yangtze River valley. The Chairman expressed to the team his lifelong belief that swimming in the nation's rivers would cultivate the Great Leap spirit of dauntlessness and a will to struggle against all obstacles. "Swimming against the river current," Mao told them, "is a good way to strengthen will and courage. We must keep away from swimming pools. Isn't it possible to make use of the many rivers of our country for swimming? Isn't it possible for 300,000,000 of our population of 600,000,000 to swim in the rivers?"[15]

The Party Chairman's effort to transfer the activism and assertiveness of a rebellious swimmer to the tasks of economic development foundered, however, on hasty planning, the inexperience of the Party bureaucracy, resistance to large-scale communal labor by a peasantry still oriented toward family responsibilities, and the bad fortune of three years of flood and drought. Opponents of Mao's policies once again sought to reduce his political influence; and in July of 1959 a group within the Party leadership formed around Defense Minister P'eng Teh-huai to attack the Great Leap Forward effort.

Despite the deepening economic crisis, the Chairman's supporters defended his program for speeding the pace of China's economic development by having Party bureaucrats lead the peasants directly in productive labor. A leadership meeting at Lushan in Kiangsi Province defeated the Defense Minister's challenge; and Mao, in victory, stressed again to his loyal comrades the belief that physical education was the basis of political discipline, a way to prevent the Party bureaucracy from becoming an effete and exploiting ruling elite like the mandarins of traditional times. Mao invoked for his supporters a passage from a classical text:

> The Prince of Chu Kingdom was ill, and a visitor from Wu Kingdom went to enquire after his health. [The visitor] denounced the decadent upper ruling class: "Well, to travel in a sedan chair or a carriage is to atrophy your limbs. To live in a magnificent and cool palace is the medium of cold and fever. To keep beautiful girls with white teeth and crescent eyebrows is to destroy your sexual health. To take rich foods is to get ulcers for your stomach." These words [added Mao] are truths good for ten thousand years. At present, with our country being under the leadership of the Communist Party, all the intellectuals and working personnel of the Party, the government, and the army must do some labor, including walking, swimming, mountain climbing and calisthenic exercises . . . not to mention going out to the countryside to participate in such still more concrete labor as farming. In short, we must exert our efforts and oppose the rightist political deviation.[16]

Despite Mao's successful defense of his economic policies in 1959, the Great Leap economic crisis which persisted into the 1960s further eroded the Party Chairman's authority. Long-time comrades continued to pay verbal respect to Mao even as they resisted his policies in implementation. The Party press began to carry articles which engaged in veiled ridicule of Mao for acting like an impetuous and dictatorial emperor of old.

It was in such circumstances that the strain of rebelliousness which has been an enduring element in Mao Tse-tung's personal style was stimulated anew. Only now Mao was an elder in his seventies, of uncertain health, and facing the prospect of eventual departure from the worldly scene. How could he preserve the legacy of his life's struggle to transform China's ancient ways in the face of Party opposition to his policies?

Mao's answer combined a search for political support from China's younger generation with that willingness to assert himself against authority which, as a young man, he had discovered in the act of swimming. In July of 1966 Mao once again made a public swim in the Yangtze and called on China's youth to follow him "and advance in the teeth of great storms and waves" in a struggle against "re-

visionists" within the Party bureaucracy. Mao's hope was that in the ensuing Cultural Revolution conflict, a younger generation untested in political combat would come to maturity:

> No one has ever learned to swim just by standing on the shore and reading about one or another aspect of the art of swimming. The same is true of making revolution. You [Red Guards] must take part in actual class struggle, master the laws governing revolution in the storm of class struggle and learn the art of swimming in class struggle.[17]

As the Chairman thus launched his Cultural Revolution assault on opponents of his policies, he told supporters at a leadership meeting, "I think it is a good thing to shock people [ch'ung-yi-hsia]. I thought about it for many years, and at last came up with this idea of the shock [of the Cultural Revolution]."[18]

冲 一 下

Mao's description of his effort to "shock" a sense of revolutionary purpose back into an increasingly bureaucratized and cautious Party organization used the Chinese character *ch'ung* with the two-stroke ice radical. His phrase implied shock in the manner that a man would be shocked by having a bucket of ice water thrown on him. Thus Mao, who as a teen-ager had rebelled against paternal authority by learning to swim, who had developed his sense of audacity and will-power by taking ice-water baths,[19] brought his career full circle in the Cultural Revolution rebellion against resistant Party authorities.

Did Mao's Cultural Revolution in fact shock a sense of activism back into the Chinese Communist Party? The course of events since the Chairman's 1966 swim in the Yangtze does not provide a certain answer. The Cultural Revolution was successful for Mao to the extent that it removed from power those "revisionist" leaders who had opposed his policies. Yet the rivalries which divided the Chairman's Red Guards indicate that China's younger generation did not have the political discipline which Mao saw deriving from "swimming" in the icy currents of political combat; and the factional conflicts which have continued to rend the leadership have left an uncertain future for Mao's activist policies.

At the same time, however, China is not simply returning to her traditional past, for younger generations—unlike their Confucian forebears—are being raised in an evolving society where swimming and physical competition are part of a new life style oriented toward the nation rather than the family, toward innovation rather than the uncritical acceptance of ancient ways. Perhaps these new generations will embody in their approach to life elements of a revolutionary culture initiated by Mao Tse-tung, who dared to swim against the tide of China's Confucian tradition.

Contra

矛盾

In traditional times the highest hope of each imperial scholar-official was to administer his district so that it would be free of all social conflict. The Confucian ideal of the perfectly ordered society, which Chinese philosophers call *ta t'ung,* or "the great harmony," served as a model state of social tranquillity in which each individual was cared for within the social bonds of filial piety —the ties of loyalty and responsibility linking father and son, elder and younger brothers, husband and wife, friend and friend, and the ruler and his ministers. Confucian political thinking was "linear" in that it assumed that if everyone in society accepted his proper place—as defined by family relationships and social obligations—

> Let the states of equilibrium and harmony exist in perfection, and a happy order will prevail throughout heaven and earth, and all things will be nourished and flourish.
> —"The Doctrine of the Mean"[1]

The Duke Ching, of Ch'i, asked Confucius about government. Confucius replied, "There is government when the ruler is a Ruler [because he acts as a Ruler should act], when the minister is a Minister, the father is a Father, and the son a Son."

"Good," said the Duke. "Indeed, if the ruler is not a Ruler, the minister not a Minister, the father not a Father, and the son not a Son, then even though I might have the grain [tax], would I be able to eat it?"
—"The Analects of Confucius"[2]

then lines of authority would be clearly drawn, there would be no "confusion," and social conflict would be eliminated through mutual care and mutual respect.

In reality, of course, Chinese society did have its interpersonal rivalries; its village conflicts and bandit violence, and periods of pervasive disorder. The times of "great harmony" under the powerful dynasties—the Han, Sung, T'ang, Ming, and Ch'ing—only gave greater contrast to the "confusion" and bloodshed of the Warring States period of pre-Confucian times and the warlord era of the early years of this century, as well as earlier periods of peasant rebellion and nomadic invasion. There was a reality to the historian's concept of dynastic cycles, of alternating periods of peace and stability, and then violence and social chaos.

A long time has elapsed since this world of men received its being, and there has been along its history now a period of good order, and now a period of confusion.
—"The Works of Mencius"[3]

When the great Tao is forgotten,
Kindness and morality arise.
When wisdom and intelligence are born,
The great pretense begins.

When there is no peace within the family,
Filial piety and devotion arise.
When the country is confused and in chaos,
Loyal ministers appear.

In the pursuit of learning, every day something is
    acquired.
In the pursuit of Tao, every day something is dropped.
Less and less is done
Until non-action is achieved.
When nothing is done, nothing is left undone.

The world is ruled by letting things take their course.
It cannot be ruled by interfering.
—Lao Tzu, *Tao Te Ching*[4]

The contradictions and conflicts in life did find expression in some of China's philosophical traditions, most explicitly in the Taoist concepts of *yin* and *yang,* interrelated yet conflicting forces of darkness and light, evil and good, female and male. Taoism emphasized the ironies and tension inherent in social institutions, although it idealized not involvement in worldly affairs but ascetic withdrawal and "non-action" (*wu-wei*). The Taoist paradox was the belief that man could achieve a special, almost mystical, power to control events through a nonassertive effort to place himself in harmony with the natural forces of the universe. In contrast, however, the philosophy which dominated China's political tradition, Confucianism, sought rule through elite consensus and hierarchical ordering of authority relations, not popular involvement in public affairs and institutionalized political conflict.

It has only been in recent times, under Communist Party influence, that a philosophy of conflict has influenced China's predominant political culture. The Marxist-Leninist concepts of dialectical materialism and class struggle have held for many Chinese a greater sense of reality than Confucian harmony. Particularly for those reared in the May Fourth era, reality has been China's time of troubles surrounding the collapse of the Ch'ing dynasty, warlordism in the 1920s, the Japanese invasion in the '30s, and the civil war between the Nationalists and the Communists. Mao Tse-tung is only the most influential member of a generation that rejected the Confucian tradition in favor of a doctrine of struggle and change. Inspired by the Marxist dialectic, Mao developed a philosophy of social change in which progress resulted from the playing out of "contradictions." As he wrote in 1937:

Changes in society are due chiefly to the development of the internal contradictions in society, that is, the contradiction between the productive forces and the relations of production, the contradiction between classes and the contradiction between the old and the new; it is the development of these contradictions that pushes society forward and gives the impetus for the supersession of the old by the new. . . . This dialectical world outlook teaches us primarily how to observe and analyze the movement of opposites in different things and, on the basis of such analysis, to indicate methods for resolving contradictions.[5]

While Mao's perspective reflects Bolshevik influence over the development of the Chinese Communist movement, his thinking has been firmly grounded in the social and political realities of Chinese life. In describing the origins of class struggle in China, Mao once observed, "The Chinese bourgeoisie and proletariat, seen as two specific social classes, are newly born; they have been born from the womb of feudal society, and have matured into new social classes. They are two mutually related and mutually antagonistic classes; they are twins born of old Chinese society."[6] This family imagery in a discussion of class conflict is one indication of Mao's sensitivity to social tensions embodied in the "harmonious" Confucian society in which he was reared. Where the scholar-officials sought to deny legitimate expression to social conflict through the doctrine of filial harmony, Mao and his cohorts have attempted to draw on class and interpersonal tensions in promoting revolution. They have stimulated "class struggle" among those who are "mutually related and mutually antagonistic" as a way of resolving "contradictions" and promoting social change.

One way of analyzing the history of China's twentieth-century revolution is to identify the major social and political contradictions which have been at the center of conflict and change in any given period of time. At the turn of the century it was the contradiction between elderly, Confucian-oriented officials attempting to preserve dynastic rule, and a new generation of youthful intellectuals seeking to bring about a revolution in culture and politics. In the 1910s it was the conflict between imperialistic foreign powers seeking economic and political influence in China, and an increasingly nationalistic youth and merchant class. This contradiction was to endure in the struggle against invading Japanese in the 1930s and '40s, in the two decades and more of hostile confrontation with the United States, and in the Sino-Soviet dispute of recent times.

The development of the Chinese Communist movement can be seen in terms of contradictory policies and leadership styles advocated by rival Party leaders. Mao Tse-tung's revolutionary strategy of a protracted peasant-guerrilla struggle from rural base areas contrasted with the approach of other Party leaders in the 1920s and '30s who advocated urban insurrection supported by the industrial workers as the basis for gaining power. "United front" policies for resisting the Japanese were another source of conflict within the Party. And after 1949, contradictory leadership "lines" regarding national social

Continued on page 127

Never before has our country been as united as it is today [1957]. . . . However, this does not mean that contradictions no longer exist in our society. To imagine that none exist is a naive idea which is at variance with objective reality. We are confronted by two types of social contradiction—those between ourselves and the enemy and those among the people themselves . . .

In ordinary circumstances, contradictions among the people are not antagonistic. But if they are not handled properly, or if we relax our vigilance and lower our guard, antagonisms may arise. In a socialist country, a development of this kind is usually only a localized and temporary phenomenon. . . .

. . . Many dare not openly admit that contradictions still exist among the people of our country, although it is these contradictions that are pushing our society forward. Many do not admit that contradictions continue to exist in a socialist society, with the result that they are handicapped and passive when confronted with social contradictions; they do not understand that socialist society will grow more united and consolidated through the ceaseless process of the correct handling and resolving of contradictions.

—Mao Tse-tung, "On the Correct Handling
of Contradictions Among the People" (1957)[7]

Continued from page 124

and economic development—emphasis on urban as opposed to rural development, reliance on intellectuals instead of the peasantry, bureaucratic rule versus mass mobilization of popular energies—came to divide Party leaders, eventually producing a struggle for succession to Mao's position as Party Chairman.

Underlying such disputes over Party policy and leadership have been certain basic contradictions shaping China's national development: Is the country's massive population an asset or a hindrance to economic progress? Can China's traditional Confucian inheritance be rapidly replaced by a "proletarian" culture? Can the Chinese economy be developed in relative isolation from contact with countries at a more advanced stage of industrialization? And will the effects of "overdevelopment" now evident in the West—industrial pollution, urban sprawl, and social alienation—come to blight China's "progress" as she develops from an agricultural to an industrial society?

Such conflicts and problems thread their way through the history of Chinese Communism, and provide some of the most meaningful concepts and images with which to interpret the development of the Chinese revolution. We explore these "contradictions" in the following pages through the interplay of visual images and policy statements by Chinese leaders.

CULTURAL HERITAGE:
CONSTRAINT TO CHANGE?

For many years we Communists have struggled for a cultural revolution as well as for a political and economic revolution, and our aim is to build a new society and a new state for the Chinese nation. That new society and new state will have not only a new politics and a new economy but a new culture.

—Mao Tse-tung, "On New Democracy" (1940)

Throughout the historical period of transition from capitalism to communism (which will last scores of years or even longer), there is class struggle between the proletariat and the bourgeoisie and struggle between the socialist road and the capitalist road. . . . Meanwhile, there still exists in society bourgeois influence, the force of habit of the old society and the spontaneous tendency toward capitalism among a part of the small producers. . . . Class struggle is inevitable under these circumstances.

—Communiqué of the Tenth Plenary Session of the Eighth Central Committee (1962)

Speaking of the internal conditions of [China], they have just grown from the old society, and in many areas the scars of the old society are still preserved. . . . In addition to remaining in the minds of the people, bourgeois ideology is ingeniously and somewhat attractively preserved in various forms (such as certain cultural heritages), and over a very long historical period, will continue to spread its influence.

—*Red Flag* commentator, "Put Ideological Work in the Primary Position" (1964)

A great revolutionary rebellion must be launched against the old ideas, old culture, old customs and old habits and all things opposed to the thought of Mao Tse-tung!

—Red Guards of Peking, in *Red Flag* (1966)

Chairman Mao points out: "Before a brand-new social system can be built on the site of the old, the site must be swept clean. Invariably, remnants of old ideas reflecting the old system remain in people's minds for a long time, and they do not easily give way." We must continue to criticize the old system and old ideas . . .

—*People's Daily, Red Flag,* and
Liberation Army Daily joint editorial,
"Forward Along the Great Road of Socialism"
(October 1, 1974)

POPULATION:
IMPEDIMENT, OR
ASSET TO PROGRESS?

The power of population is infinitely greater than the power in the earth to produce subsistence for man. Population, when unchecked, increases in a geometrical ratio. Subsistence increases only in an arithmetical ratio. A slight acquaintance with numbers will show the immensity of the first power in comparison with the second. By that law of our nature which makes food necessary to the life of man, the effects of these two unequal powers must be kept equal. This implies a strong and constantly operating check on population from the difficulty of subsistence. This difficulty must fall somewhere, and must necessarily be severely felt by a large proportion of mankind.

What then becomes of this mighty power [of population growth] in China? And what are the kinds of restraint, and the forms of premature death, which keep the population down to the level of the means of subsistence? . . . Famines . . . are perhaps the most powerful of all the positive checks to the Chinese population; though at some periods the checks from wars and internal commotions have not been inconsiderable.

—Thomas Robert Malthus,
On Population (1798)

It is a very good thing that China has a big population. Even if China's population multiplies many times, she is fully capable of finding a solution; the solution is production. The absurd argument of Western bourgeois economists like Malthus that increases in food cannot keep pace with increases in population was not only thoroughly refuted in theory by Marxists long ago, but has also been completely exploded by the realities in the Soviet Union and the Liberated Areas of China after their revolutions. . . .

Of all things in the world, people are the most precious. Under the leadership of the Communist Party, as long as there are people, every kind of miracle can be performed. . . . We believe that revolution can change everything, and that before long there will arise a new China with a big population and a great wealth of products, where life will be abundant and culture will flourish. All pessimistic views are utterly groundless.

—Mao Tse-tung, "The Bankruptcy of the
Idealist Conception of History" (1949)

IMPERIALIST AGGRESSION: SCOURGE, OR STIMULUS TO REVOLUTION?

"To Be Attacked by the Enemy Is Not a Bad Thing,
But a Good Thing."

—Mao Tse-tung (1939)

It was the enemy's gunfire and the bombs dropped by enemy aeroplanes that brought news of the war to the great majority of the people. That was . . . a kind of mobilization, but it was done for us by the enemy, we did not do it ourselves . . . Now people in the remoter regions beyond the noise of the guns are carrying on quietly as usual. This situation must change, or otherwise we cannot win in our life-and-death struggle. We must never lose another move to the enemy; on the contrary, we must make full use of this move, political mobilization, to get the better of him. . . . The mobilization of the common people throughout the country will create a vast sea in which to drown the enemy, create the conditions that will make up for our inferiority in arms . . .

—Mao Tse-tung, "On Protracted War" (1938)

Recently a Japanese merchant came to me and said, "I very much regret that Japan invaded China." I replied to him: "You are not being fair. Of course, the aggression wasn't fair either, but there is no need to apologize. If the Japanese had not occupied half of China, it would have been impossible for the entire Chinese population to rise and fight the Japanese invader. And that resulted in our army strengthening itself by a million men, and in the liberated bases the population increased to one hundred million." That is why I said to the Japanese merchant, "Should I thank you?"

—Mao Tse-tung [to visiting Frenchmen] (1964)

The First World War was followed by the birth of the Soviet Union with a population of 200 million. The Second World War was followed by the emergence of the socialist camp with a combined population of 900 million. If the imperialists insist on launching a third world war, it is certain that several hundred million more will turn to socialism, and then there will not be much room left on earth for the imperialists.

—Mao Tse-tung, "On the Correct Handling of Contradictions Among the People" (1957)

In establishing our own war industry we must not allow ourselves to become dependent on it. Our basic policy is to rely on the war industries of the imperialist countries and of our domestic enemy. We have a claim on the output of the arsenals of London as well as Hanyang and, what is more, it is delivered to us by the enemy's transportation corps. This is the sober truth, it is not a jest.

—Mao Tse-tung, "Problems of Strategy
in China's Revolutionary War" (1936)

President Nixon is fond of carrying out "izations"—"Vietnamization," "Khmerization" [i.e., "Cambodianization"] and "Laotianization." I have reminded many Americans that they concoct this and that "-ization," but can there be anything bigger than "Chinasization?" After the victory of the War of Resistance against Japan, in the four years from 1946 through 1949 the U.S. government fully equipped or reequipped a total of eight million troops for Chiang Kai-shek, and gave him all the financial aid he needed. Yet finally Chiang Kai-shek took with him to Taiwan less than a million troops. The rest had been wiped out. At that time the great majority of the Liberation Army troops used [captured] U.S. armaments. There is a photograph of Chairman Mao reviewing our troops on entering Peking, which shows him riding in an American jeep and reviewing American-made artillery and tanks. . . .

—Chou En-lai [to a British journalist] (1971)

INDUSTRIALIZATION:
SOLUTION
OR
POLLUTION?

Do you think you can take over the universe and improve it?
I do not think it can be done.

The universe is sacred.
You cannot improve it.
If you try to change it, you will ruin it.
If you try to hold it, you will loose it.

—Lao Tzu, *Tao Te Ching*

Without industry there can be no solid national defense, no well-being for the people, no prosperity or strength for the nation. The history of the 105 years since the Opium War of 1840 . . . has brought this important point home to the Chinese people.

—Mao Tse-tung, "On Coalition Government" (1945)

China has inherited a backward economy. But the Chinese people are brave and industrious. With the victory of the Chinese people's revolution and the founding of the People's Republic, and with the leadership of the Communist Party of China . . . the speed of China's economic construction will not be very slow, but may be fairly fast. The day is not far off when China will attain prosperity. There is absolutely no ground for pessimism about China's economic resurgence.

—Mao Tse-tung, "Report to the Second Plenary Session
of the Seventh Central Committee
of the Communist Party of China" (1949)

We cannot take the old path of technical development followed by various countries in the world, and go at a crawl after other people. We must break with conventions and make maximum use of advanced techniques, so that our country can be built into a modern socialist power within not too long an historical period. We mean precisely this when we talk about the great leap forward.

—Mao Tse-tung,
"The Great Leap Forward
of China" (1964)

A STRATEGY OF ECONOMIC DEVELOPMENT: INDUSTRY OR AGRICULTURE AS THE BASE?

Some comrades disapprove of our Central Committee's policy of keeping the development of agricultural co-operation in step with our socialist industrialization . . . They consider that the speed of industrialization as it is set at present is all right, but that agricultural co-operation should proceed at an extremely slow pace and need not keep up with it. . . . These comrades fail to understand that socialist industrialization cannot be carried out in isolation from agricultural co-operation. In the first place, as everyone knows, China's current level of production of marketable grain and industrial raw materials is very low, whereas the state's need for them is growing year by year, and this presents a sharp contradiction.

— Mao Tse-tung, "On the Question of Agricultural Co-operation" (1955)

Some comrades want to lower the rate of development of heavy industry. This line of thinking is wrong. We put this question to them: If we do not very quickly establish our own indispensable machine-building industry, metallurgical industry and other related branches of heavy industry, how are we going to equip our light industry, transport, building industry and agriculture?

— Liu Shao-ch'i, "Political Report of the Central Committee of the Communist Party of China to the Eighth National Congress of the Party" (1956)

As China is a large agricultural country, with over 80 per cent of her population in the rural areas, industry must develop together with agriculture, for only thus can industry secure raw materials and a market, and only thus is it possible to accumulate fairly large funds for building a powerful heavy industry. . . . We must realize that there is a contradiction here—the contradiction between the objective laws of economic development of a socialist society and our subjective understanding of them—which needs to be resolved in the course of practise. This contradiction also manifests itself as a contradiction between different people, that is, a contradiction between those with a relatively accurate understanding of these objective laws and those with a relatively inaccurate understanding of them . . .

—Mao Tse-tung, "On the Correct Handling
of Contradictions Among the People" (1957)

Comrade Mao Tse-tung has often said that there are two ways of carrying out socialist transformation and construction: one will result in doing the work faster and better; the other slowly and not so well. Which way should we take? This has been an issue. . . . On this question some comrades have clung to such outmoded ideas as, "Keeping to the right is better than keeping to the left," "It is better to go slower than faster," or "It is better to take small steps than to go striding forward." The struggle between the two ways in dealing with this question was not fully decided until the launching of the rectification campaign and the anti-rightist struggle [of 1957]. . . .

Comrade Mao Tse-tung has put forward the slogans, "Catch up with and outstrip Britain in 15 years," "Build socialism by exerting our utmost efforts and pressing ahead consistently to achieve greater, faster, better and more economical results" . . . All these calls have rapidly caught the imagination of the huge army of hundreds of millions of working people and have been transformed into an immense material force. . . .

The spring of 1958 [has] witnessed the beginning of a leap forward on every front of our socialist construction. Industry, agriculture and all other fields of activity are registering greater and more rapid growth. . . .

—Liu Shao-ch'i,
"Political Report of the Central Committee
of the Communist Party of China
to the Second Session
of the Eighth National Congress of the Party"
(1958)

INTELLECTUALS:
ASSET TO INDUSTRIALIZATION
OR
POLITICAL LIABILITY?

In China, it was among the intellectuals and young students that Marxist-Leninist ideology was first widely disseminated and accepted. The revolutionary forces cannot be successfully organized and revolutionary work cannot be successfully conducted without the participation of revolutionary intellectuals. But the intellectuals often tend to be subjective and individualistic, impractical in their thinking and irresolute in action . . . The intellectuals can overcome their shortcomings only in mass struggles over a long period.

—Mao Tse-tung, "The Chinese Revolution and the Chinese Communist Party" (1939)

I began life as a student and at school acquired the ways of a student; I then used to feel it undignified to do even a little manual labour, such as carrying my own luggage in the presence of my fellow students, who were incapable of carrying anything, either on their shoulders or in their hands. At that time I felt that intellectuals were the only clean people in the world, while in comparison workers and peasants were dirty. I did not mind wearing the clothes of other intellectuals, believing them clean, but I would not put on clothes belonging to a worker or peasant, believing them dirty. But after I became a revolutionary and lived with workers and peasants and with soldiers of the revolutionary army, I gradually came to know them well, and they gradually came to know me well too. It was then, and only then, that I fundamentally changed the bourgeois and petty-bourgeois feelings implanted in me in the bourgeois schools. I came to feel that compared with the workers and peasants the unremoulded intellectuals were not clean and that, in the last analysis, the workers and peasants were the cleanest people and, even though their hands were soiled and their feet smeared with cow-dung, they were really cleaner than the bourgeois and petty-bourgeois intellectuals.

—Mao Tse-tung, "Talks at the Yenan Forum on Literature and Art" (1942)

The mathematician Hua Lo-keng

The mass of intellectuals have made some progress, but they should not be complacent. They must continue to remould themselves, gradually shed their bourgeois world outlook and acquire the proletarian, communist world outlook so that they can fully fit in with the needs of the new society and unite with the workers and peasants. This change in world outlook is something fundamental, and up till now most of our intellectuals cannot be said to have accomplished it.

—Mao Tse-tung, "On the Correct Handling of Contradictions Among the People" (1957)

Awed by the professors—awed by them ever since we came into the cities. [Party members] do not despise the intellectuals but have an immense fear of them. They are filled with learning, while we are inferior in everything. Marxists being awed by bourgeois intellectuals! It is strange for a person to fear the professors while he does not fear imperialism. This mental attitude must be a remnant of the slave system. I cannot stand it any more.

—Mao Tse-tung, "Speech at the Ch'eng-tu Conference" (1958)

Isn't the writing of novels the fashion of the day now? The use of novels to carry out anti-Party activities is quite an invention. To overthrow a political power, it is always necessary first to create public opinion, to do work in the ideological sphere.

—Mao Tse-tung, "Speech at the Tenth Plenary Session of the Eighth Central Committee of the Chinese Communist Party" (1962)

For the last few months, in response to the militant call of the Central Committee of the Chinese Communist Party and Chairman Mao Tse-tung, hundreds of millions of workers, peasants, and soldiers, and vast numbers of revolutionary cadres and intellectuals, all armed with Mao Tse-tung's thought, have been sweeping away a horde of monsters that have entrenched themselves in ideological and cultural positions.

With the tremendous and impetuous force of a raging storm, they have smashed the shackles imposed on their minds by the exploiting classes for so long in the past, routing the bourgeois "specialists," "scholars," "authorities," and "venerable masters," and sweeping every bit of their prestige into the dust.

—*People's Daily* editorial, "Sweep Away All Monsters" (1966)

The historian Chien Po-tsan

LEADERSHIP STYLE:
BUREAUCRATIC MANAGEMENT
OR MASS MOBILIZATION?

Among our ranks . . . there are really many people who still are unable to adopt the democratic style of work; the bureaucratic style of work brought from the old society is still in existence. [Many Party members] are displeased when other people hold views which differ from their own. They like to hear only flattery but dislike criticism. . . . This kind of work style blocks the progress of our cause.

—Mao Tse-tung, "A Task for 1945" (1944)

With victory, certain moods may grow within the Party—arrogance, the airs of a self-styled hero, inertia and unwillingness to make progress, love of pleasure and distaste for continued hard living. . . . It has been proved that the enemy cannot conquer us by force of arms. However, the flattery of the bourgeoisie may conquer the weak-willed in our ranks.

—Mao Tse-tung, "Report to the Second Plenary Session of the Seventh Central Committee of the Communist Party of China" (1949)

At present, dozens of hands meddle in the affairs of the local administrations, making affairs difficult to handle. The ministries [of the central government] issue orders to the provincial de-

partments and municipal bureaus under their jurisdiction every day, although neither the Central Committee nor State Council knows anything about these orders. . . . All this should be changed, and it is necessary to work out methods for adjusting things.

—Mao Tse-tung, "On the Ten Great Relationships" (1956)

In 1956, small numbers of workers or students in certain places went on strike. The main cause of these disturbances . . . was bureaucracy on the part of the leadership. . . . In a large country like ours, there is nothing to get alarmed about if a small number of people create disturbances; on the contrary, such disturbances will help us get rid of bureaucracy.

—Mao Tse-tung, "Talk on the Question of Democratic Centralism" (1962)

[Bureaucrats] are conceited, complacent, and they aimlessly discuss politics. They do not grasp their work; they are subjective and one-sided; they are careless; they do not listen to people; they are truculent and arbitrary; they force orders; they do not care about reality; they maintain blind control . . . They promote erroneous tendencies and a spirit of reaction; they connive with bad persons and tolerate bad situations; they engage in villainy and violate the law; they engage in speculation; they are a threat to the Party and state; they suppress democracy; they quarrel and take revenge; they do not differentiate between the enemy and ourselves.

—Mao Tse-tung, "Twenty Manifestations of Bureaucracy" (1966)

What is the lesson of the revolution during [its first fifty] years? Fundamentally, it is "arouse the masses of the people."

—Mao Tse-tung, "The Orientation
of the Youth Movement" (1939)

Marxism can develop only through struggle, and not only is this true of the past and present, it is necessarily true of the future as well. What is correct invariably develops in the course of struggle with what is wrong.

—Mao Tse-tung, "On the Correct Handling
of Contradiction Among the People" (1957)

We need a rectification movement. Will it undermine our Party's prestige if we criticize our own subjectivism, bureaucracy, and sectarianism? I think not. . . . The Communist Party does not fear criticism because we are Marxists, the truth is on our side, and the basic masses, the workers and peasants, are on our side.

—Mao Tse-tung, "Speech at the Chinese
Communist Party's National Conference
on Propaganda Work" (1957)

Political work must take the mass line. It won't do to rely merely on the leaders alone. Can you [Party leaders] handle so many things? Many good and bad deeds are not visible to you, and you can see only a part of them. It is therefore necessary to mobilize everybody to assume responsibility, speak out, give encouragement, and make criticism.

—Mao Tse-tung, "Comments on Peking Normal
College's Investigation Material Report" (1965)

China's masses of workers, peasants, and soldiers and revolutionary cadres and intellectuals have started to criticize the old world, old things and old thinking on an unprecedented scale, using as their weapon the thought of Mao Tse-tung.

We criticize the system of exploitation, the exploiting classes, imperialism, modern revisionism, all reactionaries, landlords, rich peasants, counter-revolutionaries, bad elements, and rightists. . . .

In sum, we criticize the old world, the old ideology and culture, and old customs and habits which imperialism and all exploiting classes use to poison the minds of the working people. We criticize all non-proletarian ideology, all reactionary ideology which is antagonistic to Marxism-Leninism, to Mao Tse-tung's thought.

—*People's Daily* editorial,
"We Are Critics of the Old World" (1966)

Stalin and Mao Tse-tung watch as Chou En-lai signs the Sino-Soviet Treaty of Friendship, Alliance, and Mutual Assistance in Moscow, February 14, 1950

FOREIGN RELATIONS I:
NATIONALISM OR
"PROLETARIAN INTERNATIONALISM"?

The salvoes of the October Revolution brought us Marxism-Leninism. The October Revolution helped progressives in China, as throughout the world, to adopt the proletarian world outlook as the instrument for studying a nation's destiny and considering anew their own problems. Follow the path of the Russians—that was their conclusion.

—Mao Tse-tung, "On the People's Democratic Dictatorship" (1949)

Can a Communist, who is an internationalist, at the same time be a patriot? We hold that he not only can be but must be. The specific content of patriotism is determined by historical conditions.

—Mao Tse-tung, "The Role of the Chinese Communist Party in the National War" (1938)

Stalin is the true friend of the cause of liberation of the Chinese people. No attempt to sow dissention, no lies and calumnies, can affect the Chinese people's whole-hearted love and respect for Stalin and our genuine friendship for the Soviet Union.

—Mao Tse-tung, "Stalin, Friend
of the Chinese People" (1939)

The historical experience of the Soviet Union in building socialism inspires our people with full confidence in the building of socialism in China. However . . . on this question of international experience, there are different views [within the Party leadership].

—Mao Tse-tung, "On the Question
of Agricultural Co-operation" (1955)

During the latter part of his life, Stalin increasingly indulged in the cult of personality in violation of the [Soviet] Party's system of democratic centralism and the system of combining collective leadership with individual responsibility. As a result, he committed some serious mistakes . . .

—*People's Daily* editorial,
"On the Historical Experience
of the Dictatorship of the Proletariat (1956)

The root cause for the appearance of [the Sino-Soviet conflict] is actually an old one, and troubles have occurred long ago. China was not allowed [by the Russians] to carry out its revolution. Back in 1945, Stalin tried to curb the Chinese revolution. He said that we should not start a civil war and must cooperate with Chiang Kai-shek, otherwise the Chinese nation would be destroyed. We did not carry out his instruction at that time, and the revolution was victorious.

After the revolutionary victory, Stalin suspected that China was another Yugoslavia and that I would become another Tito. Subsequently, we went to Moscow to sign the Sino-Soviet Treaty of Alliance and Mutual Assistance. It took a struggle to accomplish this. Stalin was unwilling to sign the treaty, but after two months of negotiations the treaty was finally signed. When did

Stalin begin to trust us? Beginning in the winter of 1950, when the "Resist America, Aid Korea" campaign was begun, he finally was satisfied that we would not become another Tito and a second Yugoslavia.

—Mao Tse-tung, "Speech to the Tenth Plenary Session
of the Eighth Central Committee
of the Chinese Communist Party" (1962)

The leadership of the Communist Party of the Soviet Union has accused the Chinese Communist Party of "defending" Stalin. Yes, we do defend Stalin. While defending Stalin, [however] we do not defend his mistakes. Long ago the Chinese Communists had first-hand experience of some of his mistakes. Of the erroneous "left" and right opportunist lines which emerged in the Chinese Communist Party at one time or another, some arose under the influence of certain of Stalin's mistakes, insofar as their international sources were concerned . . . But since some of the wrong ideas put forward by Stalin were accepted and applied by certain Chinese comrades, we Chinese should bear the responsibility.

—*People's Daily* and *Red Flag* joint editorial,
"On the Question of Stalin" (1963)

Ours is an era in which world capitalism and imperialism are moving to their doom and socialism and communism are marching toward victory. . . . But Khrushchev, this buffoon on the contemporary political stage, chose to go against this trend . . . He nourished an inveterate hatred for the Communist Party of China . . . He spread innumerable rumors and slanders against the Chinese Communist Party and Comrade Mao Tse-tung and resorted to every kind of baseness in his futile attempt to subvert socialist China.

—*Red Flag* editorial, "Why Khrushchev Fell" (1964)

BOTH PICTURES:
Nikita Khrushchev
and Mao Tse-tung

Brezhnev, the chief of the Soviet revisionist renegade clique, frantically attacked China's Great Proletarian Cultural Revolution in his speech at a mass rally in the Gorkiy region [on January 13, 1967] and openly declared that they stood on the side of the Liu Shao-ch'i renegade clique, saying that the downfall of this clique was "a big tragedy for all real communists in China, and we express our deep sympathy to them." At the same time, Brezhnev publicly announced continuation of the policy of subverting the leadership of the Chinese Communist Party. . . . We must . . . maintain high vigilance and be fully prepared against any war of aggression that imperialism may launch and particularly against surprise attack on our country by Soviet revisionist social-imperialism.

—Chou En-lai, "Report to the Tenth National
Congress of the Communist Party of China" (1973)

Chairman Mao Tse-tung receives American President Richard Nixon in Peking, February 1972

FOREIGN RELATIONS II: REVOLUTION OR *REALPOLITIK?*

What do the Chinese Communists want? They don't want just Quemoy and Matsu; they don't want just Formosa; they want the world. And the question is if you surrender or indicate in advance that you're not going to defend any part of the free world, and you figure that's going to satisfy them, it doesn't satisfy them. It only whets their appetite; and then the question comes, when do you stop them?

—Richard M. Nixon
(in the Kennedy-Nixon TV debates, 1960)

Any American policy toward Asia must come urgently to grips with the reality of China. This does not mean, as many would simplistically have it, rushing to grant recognition to Peking, to admit it to the United Nations and to ply it with offers of trade—all of which would serve to confirm its rulers in their present course. It does mean recognizing the present and potential danger from Communist China, and taking measures designed to meet the danger.

—Richard M. Nixon, "Asia After Vietnam" (1967)

Continued on page 156

Chairman Mao Tse-tung autographs a book of his quotations for the American Robert Williams in Peking, 1967

Although U.S. imperialism has done many bad things to China and the whole world, yet the Chinese people know that only the U.S. ruling clique is bad but the American people are quite good. Among the American people, although many of them have still not awakened as yet, such people are in the minority; the vast majority are good people. The friendly relations between the Chinese people and the American people will eventually sweep away the roadblocks put up by Dulles and his like, and will develop more extensively with each passing day.

—Mao Tse-tung, "A Letter to Comrade Foster" (1959)

The rapid development of the struggle of the American Negroes is a manifestation of the sharpening of class struggle and national struggle within the United States; it has increasingly aroused the anxiety of the U.S. ruling circles. The Kennedy Administration has resorted to cunning two-faced tactics. On the one hand, it continues to connive at and engage in the discrimination against and persecution of Negroes, including their suppression with armed force. On the other hand, it is parading as an advocate of the "defense of human rights" . . .

Continued on page 157

Continued from page 154

Ten years from now the Communist Chinese, for example, among others, may have a significant nuclear capability. They will not be a major nuclear power, but they will have a significant nuclear capability. By that time the war in Vietnam will be over . . . and we are going to try to make the break-through in some normalization of our relations with Communist China.

—Richard M. Nixon (in a press conference
of January 30, 1970)

As I have pointed out on a number of occasions over the past three years, there can be no stable and enduring peace [in the world] without the participation of the People's Republic of China and its 750 million people. That is why I have undertaken initiatives in several areas to open the door for more normal relations between our two countries. . . . Our actions in seeking a new relationship with the People's Republic of China will not be at the expense of our old friends. . . . I have taken this action because of my profound conviction that all nations will gain from the reduction of tensions and a better relationship between the United States and the People's Republic of China. It is in this spirit that I will undertake what I deeply hope will become a journey for peace.

—Richard M. Nixon (press statement of July 15, 1971)

Continued from page 155

I call upon the workers, peasants, revolutionary intellectuals, enlightened elements of the bourgeoisie and other enlightened personages of all colors in the world, white, black, brown, yellow, etc., to unite against the racial discrimination practised by U.S. imperialism and to support the American Negroes in their struggle against racial discrimination. In the final analysis, a national struggle is a question of class struggle.

—Mao Tse-tung, "Statement Calling Upon the People
of the World to Unite Against Racial Discrimination
by U. S. Imperialism and Support the American
Negroes in Their Struggle
Against Racial Discrimination" (1963)

If the Soviet Union wouldn't do [said Chairman Mao] then he would place his hopes on the American people. The United States alone had a population of more than 200 million. Industrial production was already higher than in any other country, and education was universal. He would be happy to see a party emerge to lead a revolution, although he was not expecting that in the near future.

In the meantime, he said, the foreign ministry was studying the matter of admitting Americans from the left, middle and right to visit China. Should rightists like Nixon, who represented the monopoly capitalists, be permitted to come? He should be welcomed because, Mao explained, at present the problems between China and the U.S.A. would have to be solved with Nixon. Mao would be happy to talk with him, either as a tourist or as President.

. . .

In his dialectical pattern of thought, Mao has often said that good can come out of bad and that bad people can be made good—by experience and right teaching. Yes, he said to me, he preferred men like Nixon to social democrats and revisionists, those who professed to be one thing but in power behaved quite otherwise.

Nixon might be quite deceitful, he went on, but perhaps a little bit less so than some others. Nixon resorted to tough tactics but he also used some soft tactics. Yes, Nixon could just get on a plane and come.

—Edgar Snow, "A Conversation with Mao Tse-tung,"
and "China Will Talk from a Position of Strength,"
in *Life* (April 30, July 30, 1971)

YOUTH:
HOPE OF THE FUTURE?

What role have China's young people played since the May 4th Movement? In a way they have played a vanguard role—a fact recognized by everybody except the die-hards. . . . In the youth movement of the last few decades, [however] a section of the young people have been unwilling to unite with the workers and peasants and have opposed their movements; this is a counter-current in the youth movement.

—Mao Tse-tung, "The Orientation of the Youth Movement" (1939)

The world is yours as well as ours, but in the last analysis, it is yours. You young people, full of vigor and vitality, are in the bloom of life, like the sun at eight or nine in the morning. Our hopes are placed in you.

—Mao Tse-tung, "Talk at a Meeting with Chinese Students and Trainees in Moscow" (1957)

The question of cultivating successors has become increasingly urgent and important. Internationally, imperialism headed by the United States has placed its hope of realizing "peaceful evolution" in China on the corruption of our third and fourth generations. Who can say that this way of thinking of theirs is not without a certain foundation?

—*Red Flag* editorial, "The Cultivation of Successors Is an Unending Great Task of Revolution" (1964)

Youth is showing dangerous tendencies . . . youth must be put to the test.

—Mao Tse-tung [to André Malraux] (1965)

The young people are the main force of the Cultural Revolution. They must be fully mobilized.

—Mao Tse-tung,
"Talk to
Central Committee Leaders" (1966)

You [student Red Guards] have let me down, and what is more, you have disappointed the workers, peasants, and Army men of China.

—Mao Tse-tung [to Red Guard leaders] (1968)

In discussing the revision of the Party constitution, many elder comrades expressed the strong desire that we must further improve the work of training successors. Many young comrades on their part warmly pledged to learn modestly from the strong points of veteran cadres who have been tempered through long years of revolutionary war. . . . [We must promote] application of the principle of combining the old, the middle-aged, and the young in leading bodies at all levels . . .

—Wang Hung-wen, "Report on the Revision
of the Party Constitution" (1973)

WILL THERE BE SUCCESSORS
TO REVOLUTIONARY LEADERSHIP?

In the course of its struggle the Party has produced its own leader, Comrade Mao Tse-tung. . . . He has brilliantly developed the theories of Lenin and Stalin . . .

In the ten years from the defeat of the revolution in 1927 to the outbreak of the War of Resistance against Japan in 1937 . . . the whole Party fought in unity against the counterrevolutionary activities of the Trotskyist Chen Tu-hsiu clique and of Lo Chang-lung, Chang Kuo-tao and others who tried to split the Party and who betrayed it.

—Central Committee of the Chinese Communist Party,
"Resolution on Certain Questions in the History of
Our Party" (1945)

(Left to right in front row) Huang Yen-pei, Chu Teh, Ch'en Yi (in sunglasses), Liu Shao-ch'i, Teng Hsiao-p'ing, Mao Tse-tung, P'eng Chen, Ch'en Shu-tung, Chou En-lai, K'ang Sheng, Teng Tzu-hui

The question of training successors for the revolutionary cause of the proletariat is one of whether or not there will be people who can carry on the Marxist-Leninist revolutionary cause started by the older generation of proletarian revolutionaries, whether or not the leadership of our Party and state will remain in the hands of proletarian revolutionaries, whether or not our descendants will continue to march along the correct road . . . In short, this is an extremely important question, a matter of life and death for our Party and our country.

—*People's Daily* and *Red Flag* joint editorial,
"On Khrushchev's Phoney Communism
and Its Historical Lessons
for the World" (1964)

For seventeen years, there is one thing which, to my mind, has not been done properly. Originally, for the sake of state security and in view of the lessons in connection with Stalin of the Soviet Union, we created the first line and second line [within the Party leadership]. I was with the second line, while other comrades were with the first line. Now it appears that this has not done us any good. The result has been that we became dispersed. As soon as we entered the cities [in 1949] we were not concentrated, and many independent kingdoms were set up.

—Mao Tse-tung, "Speech at a Work Conference
of the Central Committee" (1966)

Liu Shao-ch'i

P'eng Chen

Liu [Shao-ch'i] and Teng [Hsiao-p'ing] conduct their activities openly, not in secret. They are different from P'eng Chen. In the past, Ch'en Tu-hsiu, Chang Kuo-t'ao, Wang Ming, Lo Chang-lung and Li Li-san all conducted activities in the open. That did not matter. But Kao Kang, Jao Shu-shih, and P'eng Teh-huai employed double-dealing tactics.

—Mao Tse-tung, "Speech at a Report Meeting" (1966)

Ch'en Tu-hsiu

Chang Kuo-t'ao

Wang Ming

Li Li-san

Kao Kang

P'eng Teh-huai

The fundamental guarantee that our proletarian state will never change its political color is to use Mao Tse-tung's thought to arm our minds, use it to unify the thinking of the people throughout China, insure that it occupies all positions and hand it on to posterity for generation after generation. Revisionism can be prevented when Mao Tse-tung's thought is grasped by the people in their hundreds of millions. In the event of the emergence of revisionism, we can rebel against it. If the father practices revisionism, the son will rebel against him.

Comrade Lin Piao is Chairman Mao's close comrade-in-arms and his best student.

> —*People's Daily* editorial, "Use Mao Tse-tung's
> Thought to Remold Our World Outlook" (1967)

Comrade Lin Piao has consistently held high the great red banner of Mao Tse-tung thought and has most loyally and resolutely carried out and defended Comrade Mao Tse-tung's proletarian revolutionary line. Comrade Lin Piao is Comrade Mao Tse-tung's close comrade-in-arms and successor.

> —The Constitution of the
> Chinese Communist Party (1969)

. . . During and after the Ninth Party Congress [of 1969], Lin Piao [engaged in] conspiracy and sabotage in spite of the admonishments, rebuffs and efforts to save him by Chairman Mao and the Party's Central Committee. He went further to start a counterrevolutionary coup d'etat, which was aborted, at the second plenary session of the Ninth Central Committee in August 1970. Then in March 1971 he drew up the plan for an armed counterrevolutionary coup d'etat entitled "Outline of Project '571'," and on September 8 [1971], he launched the coup in a wild attempt to assassinate our great leader Chairman Mao and set up a rival Central Committee. On September 13, after his conspiracy had collapsed, Lin Piao surreptitiously boarded a plane, fled as a defector to the Soviet revisionists in betrayal of the Party and the country and died in a crash at Undur Khan in the People's Republic of Mongolia.

In the last fifty years our Party has gone through ten major struggles between the two lines. The collapse of the Lin Piao anti-Party clique does not mean the end of the two-line struggle within

Lin Piao

the Party. . . . Lin Piaos will appear again and so will persons like Wang Ming, Liu Shao-ch'i, P'eng Teh-huai and Kao Kang. This is something independent of man's will. Therefore, all comrades in our Party must be fully prepared mentally for the struggles in the long years to come . . .

—Chou En-lai,
"Report to the Tenth National Congress
of the Communist Party of China" (1973)

Again, Mything

China's Communist revolution, like other great social movements of our time, has run a course from origins in the struggle of young students for justice and security in an impoverished, threatening world, through the hardships and violence of mass political combat, to the success and responsibilities of state power. Today we watch aged revolutionary leaders still burdened with the tasks of modernizing an ancient society, and seeking ways of transmitting the ideals and lessons of their lifelong struggle to successors who must carry on the unfinished work of "socialist transformation."

The founders of the Chinese Communist Party came from a generation that had rejected the words of their elders and the Confucian concepts of society. In their struggle for power they came to create new words of their own, a philosophy of revolutionary theory and practice now embodied in "the thought of Mao Tse-tung." Chairman Mao is revered as the model figure of the revolution; his writings are its distilled wisdom, guiding the transformation of Chinese society.

Those leaders who have been bold enough to challenge the Chairman's views have been isolated and held up to public criticism and ridicule.

The Museum of the Revolution [in Canton] is laid out in the circular hall of the monument to Sun Yat-sen. . . . In the museum there are photographs of the leaders of the 1925 strike, the first strike against Hong Kong . . . photographs of the peasant movement . . . the pikes with the short red tassels. . . . These photographs and these objects are mixed up with a whole folklore of the revolution . . . . They are supposed to teach revolution, and they teach martyrdom. . . . The pictures are intended not so much to make the course of the revolution intelligible as to create a past amenable to the victors. How much more effective than this propaganda would be a museum which clearly explained Mao's complex achievement to these young people around me who can only guess at it all and accept it with a vague reverence.

André Malraux, *Anti-Memoirs*[1]

As the leading "swimmer" against the tide of China's traditional culture, no one has been more conscious than Mao Tse-tung of the difficulties of transforming what is still predominantly a peasant society. Bureaucratic political management and intellectual elitism remain as threats to the active participation of China's rural millions in the process of social and economic change. The fragile plant of revolution is rooted in a people who sustain old customs and habits

"Smash the old world"

and in a land whose resources are only beginning to encourage its growth. The "contradictions" theme in Mao's philosophy emphasizes the social and political tensions, the conflicting policy choices, which China's leaders must face and deal with if they are to modernize their country successfully. Only time will tell whether the myths of revolution which are the legacy of the first generation of Chinese Communist leaders will enable their successors to sustain the momentum of social, political, and economic advance affecting the lives of nearly a quarter of mankind.

The Pendulum of America's Public Mood

If the notion of "contradictions" is a useful way of thinking about the difficulties confronting China's revolution, it is also a helpful concept for analyzing American reactions to this always intriguing country. Despite our newly improved relations with the People's Republic of China, it seems unlikely that in the 1970s we will fall prey to the exaggerated hopes of earlier generations fascinated with China that somehow our social philosophy, our religion, or our technology might help to transform this country in ways consonant with American traditions and values. Three decades after World War II we have a deeper appreciation of the difficulties of modernizing traditional societies; and the Vietnam experience has humbled our inclinations for activist intervention abroad.

At the same time, however, as the American government has moved to normalize U.S.-P.R.C. relations, we have seen once again in our public reactions to China the same exaggerated swings of mood which have been so much a part of the history of Sino-American contacts.

While Peking's Ping-pong diplomacy—which accelerated the improvement of our relations with China in 1971 and 1972—demonstrated that Chinese have now learned to play the Westerner's game, it is not at all clear that we have learned to understand the Chinese on their own terms.

A review of America's public media over the past several years shows how disturbingly persistent are the myths with which we have long interpreted China and the Chinese. In part this is a matter of enduring stereotypes derived from the history of Chinese in the United

States, a phenomenon best illustrated by a recent advertisement showing three Chinese laundrymen trying to iron the crease out of a no-press shirt. As with a contemporary radio commercial for Chinese food, American culture remains the basic referent for our visions of China.

(Forget it, fellows.)

New Vanopress is the first permanently pressed shirt that was pressed the day it was made and never needs pressing again.

The Van Heusen Vanopress™ shirt is so permanently pressed that even you experts can't iron out that crisp crease down the sleeve. Our revolutionary new development presses Vanopress the day it's made, and it never needs pressing again. Not even a little bit. No matter if this Dacron* polyester and cotton shirt is washed by hand, machine or laundry. No matter how many times. It never needs pressing again. It's the truth!

FOR PERMANENT PRESS...VANOPRESS BY

VAN HEUSEN®
YOUNGER BY DESIGN
Van Heusen and Lady Van Heusen Apparel

g. T.M. for its polyester

We continue to project our own hopes and fears onto a distant people with whom we are only beginning to re-establish contact. For example, as American exports to the People's Republic have expanded dramatically in the wake of the removal of governmental restrictions on trade with China, new life has been given to the trader's enduring dream of commerce with "400 million customers." With China turning to the U.S. for aircraft, ammonium nitrate plants, and agricultural products, the contemporary vision is of an unlimited market of more than 800 million customers. Lost in the enthusiastic response of the entrepreneur is consideration of all the factors which are likely to limit China's foreign trade in favor of policies of domestic "self-reliance" and diversified foreign risk.

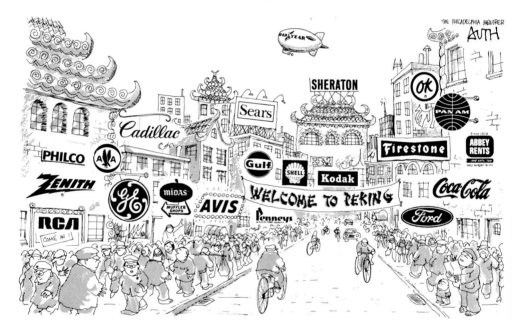

In viewing America's new China mood, one cannot but be impressed by the rapidity with which the positive images of China in the 1970s evolved from lingering Cold War perceptions of the late 1960s, replaying within only a few years' time the "good China—bad China" ambivalence of eras past. In 1967 Secretary of State Dean Rusk warned Americans of the dangers of "a billion Chinese on the mainland armed with nuclear weapons" and predisposed to a "doctrinaire and ideological adventurism abroad,"[2] thus echoing ancient fears of the Golden Horde and "yellow peril" at a time of public concern about the population explosion and atomic holocaust. In contrast, however,

Ripley's — Believe It or Not!

THE
**MARCHING
CHINESE**

IF ALL THE **CHINESE**
IN THE WORLD
WERE TO MARCH
-**4** ABREAST-
PAST A GIVEN POINT
THEY WOULD **NEVER**
FINISH PASSING THOUGH THEY
MARCHED FOREVER AND EVER!
(Based on U.S. Army Marching Regulations)

less than four years later President Nixon was to send his national security advisor Henry Kissinger to Peking on a secret mission of reconciliation. Dr. Kissinger's handshake with Premier Chou En-lai initiated efforts to erase the hostility and suspicion that had characterized the Washington-Peking confrontation of the Dulles and Rusk eras, and to build normal relations between two of the world's major powers.

This swing of public mood is all the more surprising given the image of a violent and chaotic China which had been projected in America's mass media during the Great Proletarian Cultural Revolution of the late 1960s. Our press and television portrayed student Red Guard excesses as meaningless violence perpetrated by young hoodlums brainwashed with the thoughts of Chairman Mao—an image that acquired a reality closer to home as Chinese embassy personnel stationed abroad provocatively flaunted their loyalty to Chairman Mao in ways that suggested they had taken leave of their senses. The atmosphere was such that American author Theodore White, who had interpreted China for American readers during World War II, was prompted to produce a film explaining the Cultural Revolution with the title *China, the Roots of Madness*. Yet here again,

less than five years were to pass before the pendulum of our perceptions had swung from the extremes of fear to fascination, as renewed travel and trade with China led department store merchandisers to the enthusiastic promotion of chinoiserie, and Americans rediscovered the inherent talent and culture of China's people in a captivation with the ancient medical technique of acupuncture.

Perhaps most striking among contemporary American reactions to China has been the shifting attitudes of young people unburdened by the preconceptions of their elders. China's Cultural Revolution intersected with the height of student protests against American involvement in the Vietnam War and the search for new values and life styles. By 1968 Chairman Mao, the sponsor of Red Guard rebellions, had become a folk hero on American campuses (even though by this time the Chairman had sanctioned the disciplining of his own unruly students). China seemed to many to be pointing the way to solution of America's own pressing social problems.

Ironically, however, many of Mao Tse-tung's most enthusiastic supporters in the U.S. were deflated by the July 1971 announcement that the Chairman had invited Richard Nixon to visit Peking. As it became clear that revolutionary China had decided to improve its relations with America's "establishment," new left spokesmen wrote of their "indignation at China's abrupt and irresponsible rapprochement with the United States," which had "compromised the mythic inspiration of China's revolutionary purity."[3]

To what should we attribute these great swings of public mood about China? In part they seem to reflect the well-intentioned but faddish enthusiasms of the American people, ever in search of some esoteric new frontier, yet always vulnerable to deflated disappointment when exaggerated expectations are not realized. In part they attest to the difficulties of gaining an accurate perspective on a distant and complex society which resists foreign observation and presents an ever-changing face to the world. With few Americans permitted to reside in China, much less able to break out of their own cultural constraints to meet Chinese society on its own terms, it is not surprising that our images of the country are superficial, subjective, and unsteadied by the weight of daily life. With the reality of China so distant, everyone is free to construct his own "China" with little reference to life as experienced by a Chinese.

In addition, one must consider the exaggerations of mood and image propagated by our own mass media, which only compound the swings of public fancy. How is an American to evaluate a country so variably interpreted by journalistic opinion-makers that a columnist can write in the early 1960s of a China nearing economic collapse because of "the virtual impossibility of efficient collectivized rice production,"[4] and a decade later describe prospering rural communes created by "the singular Chinese genius for capital-creation"?[5] The tendency of the press to sensationalize our images of China was described by one self-critical journalist in reviewing the shift in editorial mood which came with the Nixon administration's efforts to normalize U.S.-China relations:

> The monstrous China of the Korean conflict and the Cold War which threatened its neighbors and enslaved its own people now became the China of acupuncture, ancient art treasures, delicious food, purposeful peasants sculpting the countryside, and, of course, the brilliant, handsome witty Chou En-lai. The New York Times, the taste-maker of American journalism, no longer called the Chinese government "the most totalitarian regime of the 20th century," as it had in 1959, but instead published pieces affirming that Mao Tse-tung's doctrines had "propelled China into a continuing revolution that is producing a new society and a new 'Maoist man.' "[6]

For the general reader who would go beyond the simplified and sensationalized images of the daily press to gain a deeper understanding of China, there is little choice between the mass-marketed "I-was-there" literature of well-known general writers producing volumes on the basis of a three-week guided tour of the People's Republic, and the specialized analyses of academic writers.

Where does this leave us at a time of official efforts to establish the basis for a more normal relationship between the United States and the People's Republic of China? It would be unrealistic to assume that the factors which have made for America's changeable China moods will soon disappear, for they are sustained by public attitudes and our organizations of mass communication. Similarly, one cannot anticipate that the considerations of ideology, culture, history, and institution which lead Chinese to their particular views of America will change overnight. What one can hope for is that an interested public will seek out more searching interpretations of China, and that public officials and opinion-makers in both the United States and China will see the value of more realistic assessments of their respective societies as the basis for a stable and long-term relationship. And if normalized relations between the United States and the People's Republic of China do not come to be characterized by intimate friendship—given the fact that each country represents a distinctive culture and political tradition—at least such relations can lay aside the mythified misunderstandings and hostilities of the past to be based on an honest appreciation of our common interests, and a willingness to accept that which makes China and America each a society worthy of interest and respect.

SELECTED CHRONOLOGY

571–479 B.C.	The lifetime of Confucius.
453–221	The Warring States Period of feuding kingdoms.
221	China unified by the Emperor Ch'in Shih Huang.
206–20 A.D.	The Former and Later Han Dynasties.
618–907	The T'ang Dynasty.
960–1126	The Sung Dynasty.
1211	Beginning of the Mongol invasion of China by Genghis Khan's "Golden Horde."
1279–1368	The Yüan Dynasty of the Mongols.
1275–92	Marco Polo in China, works for the Mongol leader Khubilai Khan.
1368–1644	The Ming Dynasty.
1582	The Jesuit Matteo Ricci arrives in China; establishes residence in Peking in 1601.
1629	The Manchu invasion of North China begins.
1644–1911	The Ch'ing Dynasty of the Manchus.
1839–42	The Sino-British "Opium War," concluded by the Treaty of Nanking, which cedes Hong Kong to Britain and opens up Shanghai and other Chinese cities to English residence and trade.
1844	The United States signs the Treaty of Wanghia with the Ch'ing government, giving the U.S. "most favored nation" status in trade with China.
1850s	First period of major Chinese immigration to the U.S.

1882   The U. S. Congress passes the Chinese Exclusion Act.

1893   Mao Tse-tung born in Shaoshan, Hunan Province, on December 26.

1899   U. S. Secretary of State John Hay issues the first of the "Open Door" notes to the world powers, calling for equal access to China for all trading nations.

1900   The Boxer Rebellion against foreign influence leads to a siege of the foreign diplomatic community in July, and is suppressed by an eight-nation expeditionary force in mid-August.

1911   The Republican Revolution begins on October 10, as troops at Wuhan rebel against Manchu authorities.

1912   The Republic of China is inaugurated on January 1 with Sun Yat-sen as provisional President. He gives way on March 12 to the militarist Yüan Shih-kai as President.

1915   The "new culture movement" grows with publication of the journal *Hsin Ching Nien* (*New Youth*), edited by Ch'en Tu-hsiu. The writer Lu Hsun and Mao Tse-tung contribute articles to the journal.

1916   Yüan Shih-kai dies in June, initiating a decade of warlordism.

1917   The Bolshevik, or "October," Revolution in Russia.

1919   Chinese students demonstrate against the Versailles Peace Treaty on May 4, initiating the "May Fourth" period of political ferment.

1920   The first Comintern representative, Gregory Voitinsky, comes to China in March, meets with Ch'en Tu-hsiu, Li Ta-chao, and Sun Yat-sen.

1921   The Chinese Communist Party is founded at Shanghai on July 1 by Mao Tse-tung and others. Ch'en Tu-hsiu is elected the first Chairman of the Party Central Committee.

1923   The Third National Congress of the Chinese Communist Party, held in June, decides to ally with the Kuomintang, or Nationalist Party, of Sun Yat-sen under Comintern pressure.

Chiang Kai-shek receives military training in the Soviet Union, returns to head the Whampoa Military Academy, founded at Canton on May 1, 1924.

1927   Chiang Kai-shek, leading combined Nationalist and Communist forces in a "Northern Expedition" against warlord rule, turns his armies against the Communists and their mass organizations on April 12, establishes a "Central Government" at Nanking in the same month.

Kuomintang troops at Nan-ch'ang, acting under Communist leadership, rebel against Chiang Kai-shek on August 1. Beginning of the Communist Red Army.

Mao Tse-tung leads the unsuccessful "Autum Harvest Uprising" in Hunan Province, later flees to the Kiangsi Province border area of Ching Kang Shan to build a base for the Red Army.

1931   Chiang Kai-shek leads a third military offensive against the Red Army in July but calls off the attack when the Japanese invade Manchuria on September 18.

1934   The Long March begins in October as Communist forces evacuate Kiangsi Province under continuing attack from Chiang Kai-shek's armies.

1935   Mao Tse-tung becomes leader of the Chinese Communist Party at an emergency leadership meeting at Tsunyi, Kweichow Province, in January.

1936   Edgar Snow meets Mao Tse-tung at Pao-an, Shensi Province, in June, at the conclusion of the Long March.

Chiang Kai-shek is kidnaped at Sian, Shensi Province, in December by troops who want active resistance to the Japanese. Chiang agrees to a truce in his fight against the Communists and to form a new united front.

The Communists establish the headquarters of their new base area at Yenan, Shensi Province, in December.

1937   The Japanese begin the invasion of China proper in September.

1944   The first official U.S. government contact with the Communists begins in July, as the "Dixie Mission" of military and State Department officers reaches Yenan as an observer group.

1946   General George C. Marshall reaches China in January to begin a year of efforts to negotiate a new coalition government between the Communists and Chiang Kai-shek which would avert a civil war.

1949   The People's Republic of China is established on October 1 at Peking, with Mao Tse-tung as Chairman and Chou En-lai as Premier and Foreign Minister.

Chiang Kai-shek withdraws his government to Taipei, Taiwan Province, in November.

1950   Senator Joseph R. McCarthy, in a speech on February 9, begins his attack on "Communists" in the State Department who "lost China" for the U.S.

Mao Tse-tung and Chou En-lai sign a Treaty of Friendship, Alliance, and Mutual Assistance with the Soviet Union in Moscow on February 14.

The Korean War begins on June 25, as North Korean troops invade the Republic of Korea. President Truman "neutralizes" the Taiwan Strait with American forces on June 27.

Chinese soldiers enter the Korean War in mid-October.

1952   Land reform, begun in 1946, is completed in October. Mutual Aid Teams are formed in the rural areas.

1954   Kao Kang, head of the State Planning Commission and Party leader in Manchuria, is purged for an "unprincipled" attack on the Communist Party leadership; commits suicide in February.

Secretary of State John Foster Dulles and Foreign Minister Chou En-lai ignore each other's presence at the Geneva Conference on Indochina in July.

1955   Mao Tse-tung urges the Chinese Communist Party, in a speech on July 31, to accelerate the collectivization of agriculture by forming Agricultural Producers' Co-operatives.

1956   Soviet leader Khrushchev criticizes Stalin and his "personality cult" at the Twentieth Congress of the Communist Party of the Soviet Union in February.

Mao Tse-tung swims the Yangtze River in May and June.

1957   The mass campaign to "Let a hundred flowers bloom, a hundred schools of thought contend"—initiated in May 1956 within the intellectual community—reaches a high point of public criticism of Communist Party rule by students and intellectuals in May. The criticism is cut off in early June and is followed by an "antirightist" campaign of countercriticism of both intellectuals and errant Party members.

1958   The "Great Leap Forward" campaign to form People's Communes and rapidly increase agricultural production begins in the late summer after a series of leadership meetings.

The Taiwan Strait crisis between China and the U.S. begins on August 23 with an artillery bombardment of the Nationalist-held island of Quemoy. The confrontation abates by mid-September.

1959   Liu Shao-ch'i replaces Mao Tse-tung as State Chairman in April.

Defense Minister P'eng Teh-huai criticizes Mao's Great Leap Forward and defense policies at a leadership meeting in July; is dismissed and replaced by Lin Piao in mid-September.

Soviet leader Khrushchev attends the tenth anniversary celebration of the founding of the People's Republic of China in Peking on October 1.

1960   The Soviet Union withdraws its aid advisers and technicians from China in July and August, compounding the economic and political crisis generated by the Great Leap Forward and deepening the Sino-Soviet dispute.

1963   A mass campaign to "Learn from Lei Feng" is initiated in February, presenting a deceased yourg Army man as a model student of the "thought of Mao Tse-tung."

1964   Mao Tse-tung discusses the problem of "cultivating revolutionary successors" at a meeting of the Communist Youth League in June.

1966   Mao Tse-tung initiates the public phase of the "Great Proletarian Cultural Revolution" by swimming the Yangtze River in mid-July. The first mass Red Guard rally is held in Peking in August, and high Communist Party leaders are purged in November.

1967   Deposed State Chairman Liu Shao-ch'i is publicly criticized beginning in April.

Several of Mao Tse-tung's supporters are kidnaped by rebellious Red Guard units at Wuhan in July, in the period of maximum chaos during the Cultural Revolution.

1969   Sino-Soviet border clashes in March transform the dispute between Peking and Moscow into a military confrontation.

Lin Piao is named Mao Tse-tung's successor to Communist Party leadership at the Ninth Party Congress in April.

1970   Ch'en Po-ta, Mao's former personal secretary and a major leader of the Cultural Revolution, is purged at a meeting of the Party leadership in August.

Mao Tse-tung brings Edgar Snow atop *Tien An Men* (The Gate of Heavenly Peace) during the National Day celebration on October 1.

President Nixon toasts the "People's Republic of China" during the visit to Washington of Romanian President Ceausescu in October.

1971   China invites an American table tennis team to Peking in March.

Henry Kissinger makes a secret visit to Peking in early July to begin the process of normalizing America's relations with the People's Republic of China.

Lin Piao dies in a plane crash in Mongolia on September 13, after it is discovered he is plotting a coup d'état.

1972   President Nixon visits Peking in February to hold talks with Mao Tse-tung and Chou En-lai. The Shanghai Communiqué is issued on February 28, setting out the basic policies for normalizing relations between Peking and Washington.

NOTES

1. MYTHING THE POINT

1 Mao Tse-tung, "Report on an Investigation of the Peasant Movement in Hunan," in *Selected Works* (Peking: Foreign Languages Press, 1964), Vol. I, p. 28.

2 Cited in Harold Isaacs, *Images of Asia* (New York: Harper and Row, 1972), p. 95.

3 Kenneth Scott Latourette, *The History of Early Relations Between China and the United States* (New Haven: Yale University Press, 1917), pp. 124–25.

4 Arthur H. Smith, *Chinese Characteristics* (New York: Flemming Revell, 1894; Kennecut, 1971), *passim*.

5 Isaacs, *op. cit.,* p. 111.

6 Dorothy Jones, "The Portrayal of China and India on the American Screen, 1896–1955" (Cambridge, Mass.: M.I.T. Center for International Studies, 1955); cited in Isaacs, *Images of Asia,* p. 116.

7 Isaacs, *ibid.,* pp. 116–17.

8 *Ibid.,* p. 119.

9 See Leigh and Richard Kagan, "Oh Say Can You See? American Cultural Blinders on China," in Edward Friedman and Mark Selden, eds., *America's Asia* (New York: Vintage, 1971), pp. 3–40.

10 Isaacs, *Images of Asia,* esp. p. 71.

11 Pearl S. Buck, *My Several Worlds* (New York: John Day, 1954), p. 17.

12 See the analysis of General Stilwell's role in wartime China, including excerpts from his diaries, in Tang Tsou, *America's Failure in China, 1941–50* (Chicago: University of Chicago Press, 1963), esp. p. 74.

13 Theodore H. White and AnnaLee Jacoby. *Thunder out of China* (New York: William Sloane, 1946), p. 164.

2. EATING

1 Jan Myrdal, *Report from a Chinese Village* (London: Heinemann, 1965), p. 135.

2 *Ibid.,* p. 140.

3 "A Madman's Diary," in *Selected Works of Lu Hsun* (Peking: Foreign Languages Press, 1956), Vol. I, p. 20.

4 Quoted in Edgar Snow, *Red Star Over China* (New York: Grove, 1968), p. 135.

5 See Mao's "Talk with the American Correspondent Anna Louise Strong (1946)," in *Selected Readings from the Works of Mao Tse-tung* (Peking: Foreign Languages Press, 1967), pp. 284–85.

6 Mao Tse-tung, "Talk at the Hangchow Conference" (1965), in *Mao Tse-tung Szu-hsiang Wan-sui! [Long Live the Thought of Mao Tse-tung!]* (no publisher or date); trans. in *Current Background* (Hong Kong: U. S. Consulate General), No. 891 (October 8, 1969), p. 51.

7 Mao Tse-tung, "Report to the Second Plenary Session of the Seventh Central Committee of the Communist Party of China" (1949), in *Selected Works of Mao Tse-tung* (four vols., Peking: Foreign Languages Press, 1961–65), Vol. IV, p. 374.

8 Mao Tse-tung, "Speech at the Symposium of Group Leaders of the Enlarged Meeting of the Military Commission [excerpts]" (1958), in *Mao Chu-hsi tui P'eng, Huang, Chang, Chou Fan-tang Chi-t'uan ti P'i-p'an [Chairman Mao's Criticism and Repudiation of the P'eng, Huang, Chang, and Chou Anti-Party Clique]* (no publisher or date), p. 4.

9 "Report of the Expanded Cadre Meeting of the Ch'ang-sha Brigade," in C. S. Chen, ed., *Rural People's Communes in Lien-Chiang* (Stanford, Calif.: Hoover Institution Press, 1969), pp. 213–14.

10 Liu Yu-liang, "Eating and Drinking Is No Mere Trifle: Appendix to 'Short Commentaries Are Powerful,'" *Red Flag* (1970), No. 2; trans. in *Current Background,* Nos. 673–74 (February 20 and 27, 1970), pp. 99–100.

3. WORDS

1 Cited in Richard Solomon, *Mao's Revolution and the Chinese Political Culture* (Los Angeles and Berkeley: University of California Press, 1971), p. 49.

2 See *The Chinese Classics,* trans. James Legge (5 vols., Oxford and London: Clarendon Press, 1893–95, reprinted in Hong Kong, Hong Kong University Press, 1960), Vol. I, pp. 263–64.

3 From William Hinton, *Fanshen: A Documentary of Revolution in a Chinese Village* (New York: Monthly Review Press, 1966), p. 39.

4 See Edgar Snow, *Red Star Over China,* p. 132.

5 Mao Tse-tung, "Oppose Book Worship" (1930), in *Selected Readings,* p. 39.

6 *Ibid.,* p. 33.

7 Mao Tse-tung, "Oppose Stereotyped Party Writing" (1942), in *Selected Readings,* p. 191.

8 Mao Tse-tung, "Reform in Learning, the Party, and Literature" (1942), as cited in Stuart R. Schram, *The Political Thought of Mao Tse-tung* (New York: Praeger, 1963), p. 120.

9 Mao Tse-tung, "Report on an Investigation of the Peasant Movement in Hunan" (1927), *Selected Works,* Vol. I, pp. 47–48.

10 Mao Tse-tung, "Comment on Peking Normal College's Investigation Material Report" (1965), in *Long Live the Thought of Mao Tse-tung;* trans. in *Current Background,* No. 891 (October 8, 1969), p. 50.

11 Mao Tse-tung, "Speech at the Chinese Communist Party's National Conference on Propaganda Work" (1957), in *Selected Readings,* p. 398.

12 *Ibid.,* p. 399.

13 Mao Tse-tung, "Introducing a Cooperative" (1958), in *Selected Readings,* pp. 403–4.

14 See *Jen-min Jih-pao* [*People's Daily*], August 12, 1958, p. 1.

15 Mao Tse-tung, "Speech at the Lushan Conference" (1959); trans. in *Chinese Law and Government* (White Plains, New York: International Arts and Sciences Press), Vol. I, No. 4 (Winter 1968/69), pp. 40–41.

16 See Merle Goldman, "The Unique 'Blooming and Contending' of 1961–62," *The China Quarterly* (London), No. 37 (January–March, 1969), pp. 54–83.

17 From "Thoroughly Smash Liu Shao-ch'i's Counter-Revolutionary Conspiracy: A Brief Commentary on the 1962 Revised and Expanded Edition of *How to Be a Good Communist,*" in *Chingkangshan* (Peking), February 8, 1967; trans. in *Chinese Law and Government,* Vol. 1, No. 1 (Spring 1968), pp. 63–64.

18 Lin Piao, "Foreword to the Second Edition," *Quotations from Chairman Mao Tse-tung* (Peking: The East Is Red Publishing House, 1967), pp. vii, ix.

19 Lin Piao, "Report to the 9th National Congress of the Communist Party of China" (1969); trans. in *Survey of the China Mainland Press* (Hong Kong: U. S. Consulate General), No. 4406 (May 1, 1969), p. 25.

20 From "Comrade Chang Ch'un-ch'iao's Speech at Chiaot'ung University of Shanghai" (1968), *Tzu-liao Chuan-chi* [Special Collection of Reference Material]; trans. in *Survey of the China Mainland Press,* No. 4146 (March 26, 1968), p. 3.

21 See Chi Yung-hung, "Conscientiously Improve the Style of Writing," in *Hung Ch'i (Red Flag)*, No. 8, 1972: trans. in *Current Background,* No. 735–36 (August 29–September 5, 1972), pp. 45–46.

4. EMULATION

1 From "The Great Learning," in *The Chinese Classics,* Vol. 1, p. 372.

2 Mao Tse-tung, "On the People's Democratic Dictatorship" (1949), in *Selected Works,* Vol. 4, p. 423.

3 Liu Shao-ch'i, "The Opening Speech at the Asian and Australian Trade Union Delegates' Meeting" (November 16, 1949); trans. in *Collected Works of Liu Shao-ch'i, 1945–1957* (Hong Kong: Union Research Institute, 1969), p. 179.

4 See p. 151 for Mao's statement.

5 Mao Tse-tung, "Speech at the Cheng-tu Conference" (March 1958), in *Mao Tse-tung Tung-chih Shih Tang-tai Tsui-ta-ti Ma-k'o-szu Lieh-ning Chu-yi-che* [*"Comrade Mao Tse-tung Is the Greatest Marxist-Leninist of This Era"*] (no publisher or place of publication given; August, 1969), pp. 160–61.

6 Mao Tse-tung, "On the Question of Agricultural Co-operation" (1955), in *Selected Readings,* p. 331.

7 Mao Tse-tung, "Report on an Investigation of the Peasant Movement in Hunan" (1927), in *Selected Works,* Vol. 1, p. 46.

8 New China News Agency (NCNA), "Mao Tse-tung's Preface to New Book on Agricultural Cooperation" (January 12, 1956), in *Survey of the China Mainland Press,* No. 1209 (January 17, 1956), p. 14.

9 Ch'en Po-ta, "Under the Banner of Comrade Mao Tse-tung," *Hung Ch'i (Red Flag)*, No. 4, July 16, 1958; trans. in *Extracts from China Mainland Magazines* (Hong Kong: U. S. Consulate General), No. 138 (August 11, 1958), p. 14.

10 See Shanghai Juvenile Publishing House, *Huang Chi-kuang: A Hero to Remember* (Peking: Foreign Languages Press, 1966); *Red Flag* commentator, "Comrade Chiao Yu-lu Is a Good Example in the Creative Study and Application of Mao Tse-tung's Thought," in *Survey of China Mainland Magazines,* No. 521 (April 25, 1966), pp. 1–6. This subject of conflicting model heroes as an expression of rivalry within the leadership of the Chinese Communist Party is discussed in Solomon, *Mao's Revolution and the Chinese Political Culture,* pp. 432–49.

11 From, "Foreword to the Second Edition" of *Quotations from Chairman Mao Tse-tung,* p. iii.

12 Edgar Snow, *The Long Revolution* (New York: Random House, 1972), p. 169.

5. ISOLATION

1 As quoted in Solomon, *Mao's Revolution and the Chinese Political Culture,* p. 53.

2 *Ibid.*

3 This practice is described in Richard W. Wilson, *Learning to Be Chinese: The Political Socialization of Children in Taiwan* (Cambridge, Mass.: M.I.T. Press, 1970), p. 29.

4 See Arthur H. Smith, *Chinese Characteristics* (New York: Flemming Revell, 1894), pp. 219–21.

5 Mao Tse-tung, "Report on an Investigation of the Peasant Movement in Hunan" (1927), in *Selected Works,* Vol. I, p. 37.

6 Mao Tse-tung, "The Struggle in the Chingkang Mountains" (1928), *ibid.,* Vol. I, pp. 97–98.

7 Mao Tse-tung, "Report on an Investigation of the Peasant Movement in Hunan," *op. cit.,* Vol. I, p. 35.

8 Kuo Mo-jo, "Denounce the American War Maniacs," in *China Reconstructs* (November, 1958), p. 7.

9 See, "How to Wage 'Revolutionary Struggle': 'Teaching Material' Provided by Red Guards of Tsinghua University, Peking," in *Current Scene* (Hong Kong), Vol. VI, No. 6 (April 15, 1968).

10 See *People's Daily* editorial, "Learn from Lu Hsun's Revolutionary Spirit of Unyielding Integrity" (October 19, 1966); trans. in *Survey of the China Mainland Press,* No. 3806 (October 24, 1966), pp. 7–9.

6. SWIMMING

1 *The Classic of Filial Piety* [*Hsiao Ching*], trans. James Legge, in Max F. Müller, ed., *Sacred Books of the East* (50 vols., Oxford, England: Clarendon Press, 1879–1910), Vol. III, p. 466.

2 Edgar Snow, *Red Star Over China,* p. 132.

3 *Ibid.*

4 *Ibid.*

5 *Ibid.,* p. 133.

6 *Ibid.,* p. 147.

7 *Ibid.*

8 See Agnes Smedley, *The Great Road: The Life and Times of Chu Teh* (New York: Monthly Review Press, 1956), p. 69 ff.

9 Snow, *Red Star Over China,* p. 140.

10 Mao Tse-tung, "A Study of Physical Education," trans. in Stuart Schram, *The Political Thought of Mao Tse-tung,* pp. 94–95.

11 *Ibid.,* p. 99.

12 See, for example, Lin Piao, "Long Live the Victory of People's War," *NCNA* and *People's Daily,* September 3, 1965.

13 From Mao Tse-tung, "Swimming" (June 1956), as trans. in Wong Man, *Poems of Mao Tse-tung* (Hong Kong: Eastern Horizon Press, 1966), p. 50.

14 See Mao's discussion of this slogan in his "Speech to the Supreme State Conference" (January 28, 1958); trans. in *Chinese Law and Government,* Vol. I, No. 4 (Winter 1968–69), pp. 12–13.

15 "Chairman Mao Chats with Swimmer," *Physical Culture,* October 6, 1958; trans. in *Survey of the China Mainland Press,* No. 1886 (October 31, 1958), p. 2.

16 Mao Tse-tung, "Concerning Mei Sheng's 'Chi Fa,'" in *The Case of Peng Teh-huai* (Hong Kong: Union Research Institute, 1968), pp. 325–27.

17 *People's Daily* editorial, "Follow Chairman Mao and Advance in the Teeth of Great Storms and Waves" (July 26, 1966); trans. in *Survey of the China Mainland Press,* No. 3749 (July 29, 1966).

18 Mao Tse-tung, "Speech at the Central Work Conference" (October 25, 1966), in *Long Live the Thought of Mao Tse-tung,* pp. 41–42.

19 See Chang Tzu-chih, "A Few Aspects of the Physical Culture Life of Chairman Mao," *Wen Hui Pao* (August 10, 1958); trans. in *Survey of the China Mainland Press*, No. 1844 (September 2, 1958), p. 1.

7. CONTRADICTIONS

1 "The Doctrine of the Mean," in James Legge, trans., *The Chinese Classics*, Vol. I, p. 385.

2 Paraphrased on the basis of the James Legge translation of "The Analects," *ibid.*, Vol. I, p. 256.

3 "The Works of Mencius," in *ibid.*, Vol. II, p. 279.

4 Lao Tzu, *Tao Te Ching*, trans. Gia-fu Feng and Jane English (New York: Vintage Books, 1972), stanzas 18 and 48.

5 Mao Tse-tung, "On Contradiction" (1937), in *Selected Works*, Vol. I, pp. 314–15.

6 Mao Tse-tung, "The Chinese Revolution and the Chinese Communist Party" (1939), in *Selected Works*, Vol. II, p. 310.

7 Mao Tse-tung, "On the Correct Handling of Contradictions Among the People" (1957), in *Selected Readings from the Works of Mao Tse-tung*, pp. 350–51, 356–57, 358–59.

8. AGAIN, MYTHING THE POINT?

1 André Malraux, *Anti-Memoirs* (New York: Holt, Rinehart & Winston, 1968), pp. 346–47.

2 Department of State, Press Release ⚹227 (October 12, 1967), p. 32.

3 David Kolodney, *"Et tu China?", Ramparts* (May 1972), pp. 9–10.

4 Joseph Alsop, "On China's Descending Spiral," *The China Quarterly*, No. 11 (July–September 1962), p. 29.

5 Joseph Alsop, "A Singular Chinese Genius for 'Capital Creation,'" the Washington *Post*, January 3, 1973.

6 Stanley Karnow, "China Through Rose-Tinted Glasses," *The Atlantic* (October, 1973), p. 74.

ACKNOWLEDGMENTS

I want to acknowledge the inspiration for the conception of this study which I derived from the work of Marshall McLuhan, particularly his *War and Peace in the Global Village* (New York: Bantam Books, 1968), and from Harold R. Isaacs' study of American attitudes toward China, *Scratches on Our Minds* (New York: John Day, 1958). My own research on the symbolic aspects of the Chinese communication system and American images of China, which was largely completed between 1969 and 1971, was supported in part by a grant from the National Science Foundation.

Talbott W. Huey played a most helpful role in the process of formulating the structure of the book, in contributing certain written materials, and in identifying illustrations. Michel Oksenberg provided useful comments and suggestions on the manuscript. Carla Lennox and Francine Stoddard of Doubleday did a diligent job of locating photographs and in securing permissions for their use. Patricia A. Malone deserves credit and special thanks for research assistance and for typing the manuscript.

Particular words of appreciation are due Loretta Barrett and Mary Ellen Travis of Doubleday, and Carol Goldberg, for their editorial support and assistance in seeing the manuscript through the production process. Bente Hamann is to be credited for the outstanding design of the book.

R.H.S.
Washington, D.C.
October 1974

PICTURE CREDITS

8. AGAIN, MYTHING THE POINT?